A
Genealogical Index
of
Northampton County
Pennsylvania

- 1752-1802 -

Compiled By:
John Eyerman

Southern Historical Press, Inc.
Greenville, South Carolina

Originally printed 1925 by:
John Eyerman

SOUTHERN HISTORICAL PRESS, INC.
PO BOX 1267
Greenville, SC   29601

ISBN #978-1-63914-094-7

Printed in the United States of America

NOTES:

By the erection of new counties from time to time, old Northampton has lost
considerable of its original area; the following named townships being no
longer within its confines:
In 1811 to Schuylkill Co. Rush and West Penn Townships.
In 1812 to Lehigh Co. Heidelberg, Lowhill, Lynn, Macungie, Northampton,
    Salisbury, South Whitehall, Upper Milford, Upper Saucon and Weissenberg Twps.
In 1836 to Monroe County, Chestnuthill, Hamilton, Pocoho, Ross, Smithfield,
    Stroud and Tobyhanna Twps.
In 1843 to Carbon County, Carbon, East Penn, Lausanne, Mahoning, Mauch Chunk,
    Penn and Upper Towamensing.

The original spelling has been retained. The dates in brackets following
the name of the testor indicate the date 1st of execution: of probate of the
will: e.g. 27/12/1766-12/2/1767: execution of 27th day of Decembery 1766:
probate 12th day of December, 1767.

ABBREVIATIONS:

* His or her mark (not always an indication of illiteracy: frequently of infirmity
# Refer to Errata page 79.

bil	brother-in-law	iss	issue (children)
bro or b	brother	lds	lands mentioned
ch	children	m or mar	married
cous	cousin	s	son
co-X	co-executor	sil	son-in-law
dau or d	daughter	sis	sister
dauil	daughter-in-law	sisil	sister-in-law
dil	idem	stepdau	step-daughter
fil	father-in-law	mens	mentions
gdch	grand-child	mil	mother-in-law
gddau	grand-daughter	steps	step-son
gds	grand-son	W (capital)	witness
Godch	God-child	w (small)	wife
Goddau	God-daughter	wid	widow
Gods	God-son	X (capital)	executor

NAMES:

While many of the original names have been retained by their bearers, many
have been changed. Following is a list showing some of these changes. Curiously
enough in the same family be found various ways of spelling the family name.
Furthermore, I have met cases where members of the same family, and living
together in the same household have pronounced the family name in two or more
ways: e.g. LERCH; pronounced both LURCH and LARRICK.

AMEY from EMIG, EMICH	FOX from FUCHS	KNIGHT from KNECHT
APPLEBACH from AFFLERBACH	FRALEY from FROELICH	LEIDY from LEIDICH
ARNOLD from ARNOLDT	FRANKENFIELD from FRANKENFELDT	LOOK from LOCH
BARTHOLOMEW from BARTELME	FULMER from FELMER	MICKLEY from MICHELE
BISHOP from BISCHOFF	FUNK from FUNCK	MILLER from MULLER
BROWN from BRAUN	GRUVER from GRUBER	OVERHOLD from OBERHOLZER
CALF from KOLB	HEANEY from HENICH	OVERPECK from OBERPECK
CLYMER from KLEMMER	HECK from HECHT	RODROCK from ROTHROCK
EMERY from EMRICH	HINKLE from HINCKLE	ROOT from RUTH
EVERHART from EBERHARDT	KLINE from KLEIN	SHOEMAKER from SCHUMACHER
FISHER from FISCHER	KING from KOENIG	SHANK from SCHENCK

---more name changes:

SHEARER from SCHERER
SMITH from SCHMIDT
SNYDER from SCHNEIDER
STEELEY from STAHLE
STONEBACK from STEINBACH
STOVER from STAUFFER
SWARTZ from SCHWARZ
SWOPE from SCHWAB
VANFESSEN from VANFUSSEN
WEAVER from WEBER
WIREBACH from WIERBACH
WISE from WEISS
WOLF from WOLFF
YOUNG from JUNG

ABLE   457

1   ACHENBACH, Philip, Plainfield Twp., yeoman, 24/12/1799-21/2/1800.
Anna-Maria w. Philip, Daniel, John ch. Frederick HAHN, Michael BREITINGER
both of Plainfield. Conrad GERMANTON, Peter SIEGEL, Nathaniel MICHLER W.
ACHENBACH 687
ACKER 414 517

2   ALBRECHT, John: John SCHMIDT, Michael SCHNEIDER X. Nicholas LAROS, Abraham
SCHWARTZ W.
ALBRECHT 726 748
ALBRICHT 457
ALBRIGHT 2

3   ALEN, Jacobje: Mt. Bethel Twp. widow. 13/11/1775-19/8/1783 Derick eldest s.
Hindrick and John deceased s. Adrian s and bro Peter MIDDAGH X. Robt. HOOD,
Gerrit MIDDAGH and Benj DEPUY W
ALLEN 426 430 533
ALLISON 25 269 301 441

4   ALMAN, Henry: L. Saucon Twp., mason. 20/2/1791-6/7/1796. Mary-Barbara w.
Sarah, Maria-Elizabeth, Catharine, Ann-Elizabeth ch. also mens Peter GRUB,
s of Catherine: George TREBLE of L. Saucon, sil X. Anthony LERCH, Henry OHL
W
ALLMAN 727
ALLSHOUSE 80
ALTIMUS 665
ANDERSON 553
ANDREAS 51 63 150 164 303 370 519 542 574 734 746
ANDREWS 184
ANGELL 70

5   ANGELMEYER, Adam: L. Saucon Twp., yeoman. 15/1/1790-29/4/1790 Barbara w.
Jacob and other ch. Philip BAHL and father-in-law Jacob ESCHELMAN X
Christopher WAGNER, Peter LEITH, Stoffel RAUCH W.
ANGERMANN 235
ANTHONY 135 281 390
APPEL, Regina N. wid of John: L. Saucon Twp. 26-9-1771-19-12-1781 John
HOUSER, eldest s (not living in Penn.), gdch the ch of "my son Casper HOUSER"
d Regina (w of Philip KASS), and Barbara (w of Conrad KEENTZ). Anthony LEROG,
yeoman of L. Saucon X. Lewis GORDON, Robert TRAILL, Anthony KEENTZ W.
APPEL 61 85 258 259 280

7   APPLE, John M., L. Saucon Twp. 12/3/1764-# read 20/11/1755-16/5/1764. mens w
Regina and Godch Regina BROUT. Regina w X. Jacob FREY, Conrad WAGGONER W.
(signed APPEL)

8   ARBO, John: Bethlehem. Moravian. 10/12/1772-18/12/1772. mens his friends
Jno. FROMELT, and Matthew OTT of Bethlehem, Amatheus THRAME, Philip REITZENBACH,
Jacob HERR and David ZEISBERGER. John ETTWEIN of Christian SPRING and John BONN
of Bethlehem X. Jacob HERR and Aug. SCHLESSER W. #(read ETTWEIN of Bethlehem and
Bonn of Christian Spring)
ARBO 235

9   ARMSTRONG, William: Allenstown 16/6/1758-19/3/1760. Elizabeth w. Agnes and
Margaret ch. James KERR and James CRAIG X. James KERR and William KERR W.

10 ARMSTRONG: Northampton; yeoman. 16/2/1764-14/4/1769. Margaret w. Robert and
Elizabeth ch. David and James KERR bil. Robert YOUNG, John Lattimore and
William KERR W.
ARMSTRONG 795

11 ARNDT: Abraham: Williams Twp. 24/11/1791-24/12/1795. ch Abraham (eldest ch),
Catherine (w of), Philip, Elizabeth (w of Jacob HAGER), Jacob. mens lands of

11 ARNDT:Abraham-continued
Christopher BITTENBERGER and Jacob WILHELM, s Philip and Jacob X. Robert TRAILL, Jacob ARNDT Jr. and George IHRIE W.
ARNDT 74 83 112 169 205 219 277 326 385 411 412 457 554 587 596 621 641 647 739 744 790
ARNOLD 336 435 669
ATEN 138 463 758
AYERS 429

13 BACHMAN: Jacob senior: Weissenberg Twp. yeoman 30/4/1787-27/0/1789 Catharine w. and late widow of William SCHMETTER of Albany Twp., Berks. s Paul and Jacob X. Laurence and Nicholas X, dau Christina iss. Elizabeth iss. Susanna iss Ottilia iss. and Mary-Elizabeth.
Jacob HORNER and Nicholas SCHWATZ W

14 BACHMAN: John N., Upper Saucon Twp, yeoman. 26/9/1801-10/11/1801 Elizabeth w. ch Mary (iss Abical) Samuel X, David X and others
Abraham and Jacob BACHMAN W
BACHMAN 280 290 436 529 716 617
BACKHOUSE 717

15 BADER: George: 24/7/1771 - (?) Maria-Barbara w X "my brothers and sisters" my relatives, Philip BUCHECKER X. George LEIBERT, Johannes HERTZELL, Dewalt MACH W
BADER 29

16 BAER: Christopher: Whitehall Twp. yeoman 16/11/1784-15/8/1786 ch Jacob X and others. Peter RHOADS, Casper STERNER W

17 BAER: Jacob: Lynn Twp, farmer 27/9/1779-(?) Ann-Mary w X. ch John and Martin. deceased s Valentine had iss, one named John. Jacob MILLER, John SISER, William STUMPFF W

18 BAER: Melchior: Macungie Twp 26/2/1773-16/3/1773 Eve-Elisabeth w. 8 ch. s and dau incl Melchior (eldest) and Jacob. Anthony STALER and Leonard STEININGER X. Frank WERKS, Nicholas KLOTZ W. (a Presbyterian)

19 BAER: Peter: Heidelberg Twp. 25/3/1777 - (?) Catherine-Elizabeth w X. and Michael HOFFMAN X ch. Jacob, Johann-Henry, Johan-Peter, Samuel, Mary-Catherine, Anna-Margareth, Anna-Apolina. mens Martin SCHNERR. John-Philip SCHAEFFER, Michael HOFFMAN, Henry SCHLEBACH, Martin HORTER W
BAER 113 130 173 297 348 434 482 537 664 745
BAEHRRINGER 710
BAEST 39
BAGGE 183
BAHL 5 541
BALDAUFF 662

20 BALIET: Paul: Whitehall Twp 15/3/1777-2/8/1777 s Stephen given plantation in Towamensing Twp where Samuel SOMMENY now lives. mens s John, Paul (minor), Nicholas (minor), Mary-Magdalena W. mens plantation bt of Samuel MORRIS, and his sil Adam DESHLER, Dana HAHN, Joseph BALLIET, and Nicholas MARCH W.
BALL 541

21 BALLIET: Jacob: 22/2/1797 - 4/1/1798: Philip WALTER and Jacob and Fredk. KUNTZ W
BALLIET 20 39 124 205 572 642 697
BARLEY 536
BARKER 629
BARNET 781
BARTHOLD 326
BARTHLEMEW 152
BARTHOLOMEW 259

22 BARTON: Thomas: Perth Amboy, (N.J. 12/5/1779-10/12/1782 s of Thomas of
     Philadelphia, mercant X. mens ch of his brother Theophilus Euphane
     Whits. Margaret PelIN wid of bro Theophilus (Bethsheba); Thomas Patterson
     of Perth Amboy; Thomas B. and Hannah Tucker ch of bro Anthony: niece
     Theodosia Prevest iss: and friend William Barnet. Henry van Vleck of
     Bethlehem, Christian Lewis-Benzious and Henry van Vleck jr W. IN CODICIL:
     William Dunlap s of Samuel Dunlap of Perth Amboy and Robt. Fritz Harding.
     Bartow 231 734 739 759
     Basinger 75
23 BASLER: Jacob: Plainfield twp yeoman. 11/10/1799-4/11/1799. Maria w. ch
     Michael, John, Jacob, George, Elizabeth, Catherine, Maria and Susanna(all
     minors). mens John Rhoads of Allentown. John Rothrock and George Gold X.
     Nathaniel Micher, Abraham Metzger, John Rothrock W
     Basse 231
24 BASSEL: George: Up. Saucon twp yeoman 26/3/1790-24/10/1795 mens bro
     Zacharias: Vanentine Reinhard; E&Margaret, late w of John Stout: two youngest
     ch of George Blank george and Elizabeth). Friend George Blank of Upper
     Saucon X Christian Clymer W
     Baster 646
     Batt 569
     Bauer 540 675 746
     Bauman 578
25 BEAR: *Jacob: Alen twp yeoman. 3/10/1788-10/10/1788. ch Jacob, John, Christian,
     Anna, Barbara, Elizabeth (decd. iss), Eversena, mens lands of Rev Francis
     Peppard, Anthony Cleppinger, and Frederick Cleppinger. s Christian of London,
     Derby twp Chester Co. and David Miller of Plainfield twp sin X. James Allison,
     Hannis and Jacob Musselman W
26 BEAR: William: Mt Bethel twp 8/1/1780-17/3/1780 Mary w X. ch Robert, Thomas,
     William, Peter, Abigail, Sarah, Martha, Jane, Mary. His bil Mr John Lowry
     co-X. Thomas Purry, Asa Everitt and Margaret Everitt W
     Beard 88 324 660 661
27 BEARY: Michael: Salisbury twp 11/8/1800-6/10/1600 Eva w X. ch Magdalene (eldest
     d wf of Jacob Deffenderfer), Barbara (w of Herman Rupp), Catherine (w of
     Conrad Beaver), John X. Henry X mens land adj Jacob Berger. P. Koehler,
     J. Bieber W
     Beatie 195 221
     Beaver 27
28 BECK: George senior: yeoman 18/11/1791-1/9/1792 Christina w. ch Andrew (eldest)
     X Ann-Mary (w of Thomas Hartman ESq), Henry X, Margaret (w of John Hill),
     Ann-Elizabeth, George. Margaret's son, Henry Nagel, Fredk. Gwinner, Peter
     Ihrie, George Ihrie W
29 BECK: J. Frederick: Bethlehem. 27/9/1788-8/11/88 John Gumbold and Joseph
     Oerter of Bethlehem X mens his mother, Barbara Sybilla Beck. bro Christian
     Henry Beck; sisters Anna Sybilla Beck of Litiz, and Christina (w of Michael
     Buck of Nazareth), mens bonds of Joseph Horsfield and Felix Fenner. mens
     Samuel Bader, Francis Thomas Frederick Kushel of Bethlehem, John Hassen,
     David Michler W
     Beck 113 165 170 177 198 312 392 486 564 588 598 760 786
30 BECKER: George Ernst; Easton, yeoman. 16/12/88-7/1/1789 ch first wf Gertraut,
     John, Elizabeth Bastian, Jacob. mens dau Ann-Margaret (w of Nicholas Trexell
     of Easton), Nicholas Trexell X. Peter Shnyder, Nicholas Yohe W
31 BECKER: John: Adam. Up Milford twp 7/12/1771-3/1/1772 Catherine w X. and
     Peter Miller X had iss. Conrad Seip, Valentine Steiner W

Beckey 658
Beger 241
Beidelman 217 223 240 407 416

32 BEISEL: LudwigN Christian Spring. 10/12/1796-24/3/1797. mens Catherine
(w of Paul Mecksch) Nathaniel Mecksch, Christian Mecksch, Niels
Tellofssen of Nazareth: Ludwig, s of Matthew Muecke: Joseph Schweishaupt,
John Petersen. Nicholas Heber X. Jacob Hanke, Fredk Schmidt W

Beitelman 547
Beissel 572
Beittel 52
Belling 104 254 598
Bellisfelt 310
Bellman 228 349
Beltzius 228 54
Bender 94 276 358 662
Beninghoff 244

33 BENNINGER: (?) (?)-9/10/1794 Ulrich Benninger X Frederick Kuntz W

Benninger 40

34 BENNY: * John Richard: Whitehall twp 2/9/1758-22/2/1758 Regina-Luisa w.
bro Jacob Benny. cousin, Andreas Deemer X. John-George Smith, John-Nicholas
Snyder W. (Richard should read Rinerd)

Benzious 22
Berdly 44
Berg 289 714
Berger 263 265 346 787
Bergstressor 331
Berlin 169
Bernhard 448 799
Bernhart 172

35 BERRGHAUS: George: Gnadenhutten, Penn twp. wheelright 26/11/1773-20/08/1788.
mens Abraham, John, George, Jacob, Anna-Maria, Christian X Jacob Rubel W

36 BERTHOLL: John: Moore twp yeoman 5/11/1785-4/7/86 Maria-Barbara w X. mens
John s, elder dau Anna-Maria "now seegel", second dau Lisbeth-Margreta,
third dau Maria-Catherine, other dau Maria-"barbera". John Miller co-X.
John Hugus, And. Diemer W

Bertsch 294 406 800
Besir 65

37 BEST: *Jacob: Williams twp 22/12/1788-2/5/1789. Catherine w. ch John X,
Conrad, Ann (wf of Andrew Uhler). Christina (w of Jacob Dech) Elias Herter,
George Drum W

38 BEST: Nicholas Williams twp 8/12/1788-15/1/1779 Elizabeth-"Cathrenah w X.
mens Christian s X Nicholas s and other ch Peter Kachlein, W. Roup W

Best 71 294 554 618 650 764 800

39 BETTY: *Joseph Lehigh twp yeoman 7/6/1784-8/8/99 Anne w X. ch John, Margrata
(Haeffelfinger), Ann Ann (Sylface), Hannah (Balliet), May (Petty), John Dunn,
Henry Baest W

Betty 708
Betz 232

40 BETZELL: Godfrett: Lynn twp 23/4/1770-26/8/1772 Anna Barbara w. Isaac s
Matthias Probst X and W. Anthony Deninger, Geo. Michael Kunz W

Beyer 241 422 448 513 761 799

41 BEYL: ⸶Balthaser: Wm. and Peter Schaeffer W
    Beyl 81 241 262 304 354 376 587
    Bibighause 479
42 BIEBER: Jacob Salisbury twp (?)-12/11/1798 Jacob and John Bieber X. George
    H. Martz, Peter Kohler W
    Bieber 27 125
    Biechy 501
    Bigely 157
43 BIEGY: Otto: 23/1/1760-25/3/1760. Anna-Maria w X. Frederick Russi guardian
    of Anna-Magdalena and Charlotte. mens Jacob, Bernhard Miller, Anthon Lerch W
    Bietschman 231
    Bietz 761
44 BIGGER: Peacock: Charlestown, Cecil Co. MD. 6/11/1753-(?). mens Redmond
    Conyngham, merchant of Philadelphia (50 pounds), Rev. Samuel Finley, Jacob
    Shoemaker of Phila. and 44's wife Margaret. Benjamin Bradford, Andrew-
    Nathaniel Berdley W
45 BILLMAN: Jacob: Lynn twp 16/1/1779-(?). eve his w X. and iss all minors.
    bil Henry Ruprecht Philip Sitler coKX. Ph. Sutler, Mathias Probat W
    Billman 287 771
    Bingham 90 457
46 BIRD: John, Allentown, gentleman. 14/9/1799-28/6/1600 William s. mens sister
    Mary Shrigley of London, Eng. late uncle James Clegg of Leghorn, Italy;
    Richard Taylor, tea merchant, of Bristol, Eng. friend Edward Mott X of Easton,
    Pa. friend Thomas Mawherter: Michael Schrader of Alen Town, blue-maker and
    dyer; his bros Thomas and William. Robert Young, Henry Howell, Margaret
    Foltz W
    Bishop 680
    Bittenbender 11 82 343 475 618
    Bitz 172
    Blackley 170 301
47 BLANK: George, Upper Saucon, yeoman 20/10/1798-14/3/1799 ch George X, Barbara,
    Magdalen, Elizabeth. gds Elizabeth and Catherine Gerhardt. mens lands of
    late John Tooly; Andrew Keck and Michael Herlacher co-X. John Herlacher,
    Abraham Snyder and Peter Morey W
48 BLANK: Christopher, Whitehall twp yeoman. 5/5/90-15/4/1793 Elizabet w X. mens
    Eve-Mary "and other ch all daugh". Friend Michael Herlacher, co-X. Peter
    Rhoads, Conrad Mark W
49 BLANK: Adam, Salisbury twp 1765/1765. Margaret w. ch George-Adam, Christopher
    George, John (apparently decd, but iss), Ann-Margaret, Catherine, Anna-
    Elizabeth, George Blank and Peter Boger X. Henry Noch, Peter Knappeley W
    Blank 24 76 187 356
    Blass 538
    Bloss 207 313 608
    Blum 254 424 768
50 BOBBENMEYER: Stephen, 10/4/1790-19/6/1790. mens Conrad Klein, Jno. Vogt. Adam
    Heckman and Conrad Walter
    Bock 287
    Boeckel 183 202 322 386 422 486 524
    Boehler 52 183 245 297 426 439 524 525 556 585 YER UER 634 734
    Boehm 81 262 121 775
    Boehner 797
    Boeli 694

51 BOEMPER: Abraham, Bethlehem, silversmith. 2/4/1785-25/2/1793. mens gddau as
    follows- Joanna (w of Nicholas Shaeffer), Eleanor (w of Ludwig Huebner),
    Cornelia (w of Abraham Andreas) Beater (w of Ansen Smith), Rachel (w of Conrad
    Gerhard). mens step-dau Eleanor Andreas; gddau Philipina (w of John
    Weinland of Hope, N.J. iss); gds Abraham Boemper. Johanna and Cornelia
    decd. at time of will. Abraham Andreas of Bethlehem, silversmith X and guar.
    Adam von Erd, John Hassen and John Merck W
    Boemper 79 303 370 604 620
    Boerheck 357 395 701 730 785

52 BOERKEL: Frederick, Bethlehem, farmer. 12/10/80-7/11/1780 Barbara w X. 7 ch
    Tobias X, George Frederick (youngest s), Christian, Elizabethm Mary, Anna
    (w of Peter Fredk. Raushenberger), Anna-Rosina (w of Peter Rose). mens
    Rev. Nathaniel Seidel; Francis Thomas, joiner of Bethlehem (guar of George-
    FredK). John Hasse, ch Freierick Reitzel, Wilhelm Boehler 2 W
    Boerlin 678
    Boersteeter 178
    Boger 49 27

53 BOGERT: Peter, Salisbury twp yeoman 3/8/1797-29/12/1800 Jacob s X. Catharina
    d (w of Frederick Mohr). mens George Savitz, Peter Rhoads, Peter Shano (?)
    Bohanner 133
    Bolzer 182

54 BOLTZIUS: Godlich, Northampton twp M.D. 28/8/88 13-7-1791 mens Anna-Maria (w of
    George Witman) Gods George Godlieb. Catherine d of John Neiper. Charles
    Deshler, John Keiper X
    CODICIL: (?)-13/7/1791. Geo. Shiver. J.Horn W
    Boltzius 140
    Bommand 469

55 BONN: John, Bethlehem. 31/10/1795-20/1/1797 mens George Golkowsky X, Matthew
    Wetzel X. friend Andrew Basse and his w Christina, H.A. Sweenitz, Treas.
    S.G.H.: nephew, Jacob Bonn, s of bro Jacob Bonn of Salem, N.C.: gdch
    Samuel Reichel. Charles-Anton van Vleck, s of Jacob van Vleck.
    Bonn 8 231 309 424 630

56 BORHEK: John Andrew, Bethlehem. (?)-28/7/1791. Paul Weiss and Jahn Hasse W

57 BORGER: *Nicholas: Chestnuthill twp 15/1/1791-11/6/1791. Andrew Correll W
    Borger 174
    Borman 258

58 BOROMAN: James, Mt Bethel twp 28/6/1770-3/4/71 Mary w X ch James and Andrew.
    James Hutchinson, John Sillaman co-X. Anthony Moore, Hugh Patterson and
    William Moore W
    Bortz 131 337
    Bossert 275 338
    Bowman 411 469 533 566
    Bower 483
    Bowrin 182

59 BOYD: *William, Allen twp county of Bucks 30/1/1752-20/6/1758 Joan w. ch
    Robert and Thomas. guar George Grav. John Boyd and John Cook X. John Brown,
    Hugh Wilson and Thomas Thomason W

60 BOYD: John, Forks of the Delaware, yeoman 11/1/1759-12/3/1759 Elisabeth w and
    four s and three dau. Samuel Brown and James and Robert Young X. George
    Sharp, James Drake W
    Boyd 141 234 269 340 723 794
    Boyer 627 687

Bradford 44
Brady 567
61 BRANDT: *William, L. Saucon twp yeoman. 4/4/1755-26/5/1755 Madlin w. ch
    Ragena and Madlen. Michael Schlayer and John Apply W
62 BRATZ: John George, Hamilton twp yeoman. 5/1/1771-5/12/1778 Margaret w X.
    ch George (minor), Catherine, Margaret, Eve, Resinah. Nicholas Ramstaine W
Braucher 68
63 BRAUMILLER: *Ludwig, 30/3/1795-1/12/1801. mens Adam Loeb, Marton Andreas
Braun 435
Brauss 246 233
Breecton 229
Breinig 196
Breisch 771
Breitinger 1
Brenner 774
64 BRUNNER: Appelenia. (?)-13/6/1773. To "Henry Runfield, everything: do make
    make my last will and it is hereby made sure that Henry Rumfield shall have
    all that I leave behind: further, I did send some writing to Lewis Klotz
    with Michael Smith, which I now repent that I did so; I say hereby that
    Lewis Klotz shall give the same writing which I sent him by Michael Smith to
    Henry Rumfield and this is my last "will and testament" John Newcomer and
    Philip Soeller W
Bress 744
Bruesch 635
Brey 146
Bricius 662
65 BRINCKER: *Anreas, L. Saucon twp yeoman. 12/3/1764-12/5/1764 Sarah w X. ch
    Olrig (Ulrich)X Henry, Andreas, Jacob. dil Elisabeth Beesir.
    Anthony Lerch and Rudolph *Oberly W
Brinen 115
Briner 299
66 BRINGH: John, L, Saucon twp weaver 28/1/1760-31/3/1760 mens Regana w and ch
    John and Daniel. Philip Ralph; Snider et al W
67 BRINK: Henry, Up Smithfield twp 1/4/1797-1/5/1797 mens Nelly w. bros Manuel
    junior, J Samuel, Johnathan (had s Henry)M had father
    and 5 bros. Manuel B. Jr and Janes Green X Moses Brink and Mary *Marks 2W
Brink 652 720 626
Brinker 526
Brintz 227
Brittain 758
Britten 663
68 BROBST: John, Limetown twp yeoman 30/6/1792-18/9/1792. Barbara w X. ch
    Catherine, Maria, Martin (eldest s minor), John, Peter, Ferdinand, Jacob,
    Christina, Christian and Elizabeth (10). Cousin John Brobst and bro
    Valentine Brobst of Limetown X and guard. Christian Braucher and Jacob
    Fetterhoff W
Brobst 300 523 551 635 641 725
Brocksch 328 362 618
Brod 472
69 BROEDER: Wendel, allen twp farmer 20/2/1786-7/4/1786 Elizabet w X. ch Philip
    X and other ch(minors), Lorens, Philip, Henry, Adam, Chris-(omit),
    Chatrina, George, Mary, Therethea, Jacob; John-Frederick and Wilhelm Creutz W

70 BROADHEAD: Daniel, L. Smithfield twp Esquire. 24/6/1755-5/3/1755. Esther
w X. ch Charles,Garret, Daniel, John, Luke, Ann (Carton). James Burnside
of Bethlehemtwp. John Hones of L. Smithfield, blacksmith, and Ephriam
Colver of L. Smithfield as trustees and guardians William Angell, William
Edwards W
Brodhead 188 735
Brodt 159
Brorheck 363

71 BROTZMAN: *John Frederick, 3/4/1760-3/5/1760. Maria-Barbara w. ch Jacob
(eldest s), Adam, f Frederick, Johannis, Nicholas, Barbara (w of Paul-
Kiessers). Nicholas Best, Matthew Bruch and Jacob Ruch W
Brotzman 397
Broudenbock 767

72 BROUSS: Catherine: Northampton twp seamstress. mens sil Jacob Probst: gddau
Catherina (w of Dr James Smith). bro Christian Haggenbuch X Peter Rhoads
and George Graff W
Brout 7

73 BROWN: John 24/5/1798-7/6/1798. Elizabeth w. ch Lettice, Polly, Samuel, mens
lds of Abraham Mensch and George Woolf. Moses Hemphill and James Ralston X,
Lettice Ralston and Joseph Burk W

74 BROWN: James, Allen twp yeoman 17/7/1800-15/9/1800. mens his mother: "John
Hays s of Jas. "Hays and my sis Sarah: sis Esther w of Robt. "Craig (had
Mary); James Brown s of bro William and Jane: James Craig s of William and
"Elizabeth Craig; William Herron s of Thomas "Herron and Jame; Samuel Herron
s of Thomas "Herron and Jane; bro Joseph and two s "William and James;
Samuel s of decd."Bro John: Jane Brown d of bro William; and "bro Robert:
Sarah w of William Starling" Bro Joseph Brown, John Arndt and George Palmer
X. William Hall, Saml. McNeill, and Samuel Landis W

75 BROWN: John-George Allen twp 30/1/1752-20/6/1758. Joan w. ch Robert and Thomas.
Guar (should read 22/4/1758-24/5/1758: Maria-Anna w. and iss. Jost Vollert,
David Basinger W)
Brown 59 60 115 188 219 269 272 395 457 545 546 708
Bruch 71 640

76 BRUNNER: Henry, Up. Saucon twp 27/1/1770-23/2/1770. Magdalena w X. ch John
(eldest), Henry, Margaret (w of Danl. Horlacher), Reinard, Andrew, Peter,
Catherine, Abraham and Elizabeth mens his neighbors Jacob, Morry, and George
Blank Xs. J. Oakley, And. Erdman, Mich Seider W
Brunner 606
Buche 305
Buckhecker 15 280 493 502
Buchman 14 623 648
Bulisher 254
Bulman 320
Bunce 703
Buninger 70

77 BURCKHALTER: *Ulrich, Whitehall twp yeoman 31/7/1761-16/4/1762. Barbara w. ch
Mary-Elizabeth, Catharine, Magdalena, Barbara, Margaretta, Dorothea. s Peter
X. John Nicholas Snyder W
Burckhalter 121 614 629 697

78 BURGER: Daniel, (prob. bet. 1774-77) mens sil Adam Thomas (nar Ann-Mary,
Heidelberg twp 22 Jan 1774); sil Lawrence Wehr (mar Juliana Burger and iss);
gds John Thomas; s(?) Casper Peter, Abraham Shellhauer, George Geiger W

Burk 7% 399 400
Burnet 22
79 BURNSIDE: James, Littlelot. 11/10/1752-1/9/1753 Mary w X. "Mankas Creek
where I live " mens A. Boemper, J. Oakly, Timy, Horsfield, and Abraham
Buenninger. Elizabeth Payne W
Burnside 70
80 BUSH: Henry, the elder, Easton, tavernkeeper. 3/11/1780-9/11/1780. Ann-Mary
w X. "six living ch" and 2 ch of decd s Frederick. Michael Yohe, Easton, co-
X. Herman Schnyder, Henry Allshouse, Robert Traill W
81 BUS(C)H: Ludwig, Up Saucon twp yeoman. 3/9/93-16.9/1794. Anna-Catharina w.
ch Catharina (Eschbach), Daniel, Peter X, Margaret (Stout), Anna-Maria
(Graeff), Barbara (Sleider), sil John Eschbach co-X. "bought land here
9/12/72" mens land of John Newcomer (W), Philip Boehm, Henry Mauer. gddau
Catherine Sleider d of my d Barbara w of Valentine Sleider, John Hasse,
William Schaeffer W
82 BUSH: George, Easton 20/1/1777-27/7/1779. Christina w X. ch Henry X,George
X, John X, Christian, Catherine; Chris, Bittenbender and Peter Ealer W
Busse 55
Butler 411 626 721
83 BUTZ: Michael, Forks twp 13/6/1779-30/7/1779 Elizabet w X. Jacob eldest s
given lda in Nolton, Sussex Co. N.J. where he now lives. mens Henry,
Christian, Peter, George each 100 pounds. 13 ch Catharina, Jacob, Charlotta,
Henry, Christian, Elizabeth, Margareth, Peter, George, Michael, Coecelia,
Abraham and Mary. mens Catherine (w of John Sipperlein) given plantation in
Nolton. bgt lds in Nolton of Jacob Staehly. Christian s X and Benjamin Siegal
of Bucks X. John Arndt, Jacob Shoemaker, McOdenwelder W. Inventory 2991
pounds. (see Eyerman: Genealogical Studies)
Butz 268 310 338 456 763 739 740
Cady 491
Calbreath 482 476
Cally 552
Calver 231
Calwell 795
84 CAMER:(Kemerer) Friedericl: Up Milford twp 6/11/1778-23/11/1778 Rossina w. ch
Henry (eldest), Jacob, Rossina, (w of George Reiss), George X, Christina
(w of Conrad Neymeyer), Friederick, John. Ludwig Stahler of Up Milford co-X.
Adam Schuller. Peter Kocken W
Campbell 758
Cane 494
Canterbury: Archbishop of 229 532
85 CAPIS: (Cappes) Henry, Saucon twp 21/12/;782-(?). Anne-Mary w X. Christina and
Catharina ds. gdch Anna-Mary. Paul Appel co-X. Conrad Fegelman, Michael
Ernst W
Cappes 85
86 CARNAGHAY: William, senior, Mt. Bethel twp. 18/6/1774-17/8/1774. Jude w X.
ch William X, Alexander, John, Robert, Margaret, Esther, Jude, Site. John
Mack and Benjamin Goodwin of Mt Bethel co-x Thomas Parry, Zenas Everitt and
Abraham Everitt.W
87 CARRUTHERS: William allen twp. 19/12/;776-18/8/1777. Mary w X. and William
McNair of Allen twp X. mens his bro Samuel minor ch (William, Samuel,
Margaret). Robert Lattimore, Neigel Gray, John McNair W

88 CARRUTHERS: Samuel, Allen twp weaver. 2/9/1769-9/10/1769 Margaret w X. "two
    minor s had 2 half s sisters Elizabeth and Mary McEnhyre. mens John Ralston;
    bro William C. X. Arthur Lattimore, James Clendinin, Robert Beard W
    Carruthers 102 564 581 743
    Case 6
    Castard 720
    Chambers 720
    Chapman 148 180
    Chestnor 110 111 411 719 733
    Chilcot 527
    Christ 91 104 142 163 177 178 185 224 339 413 420 487 503 539 577 600 606 622
89 CHRISTMAN: Henry, Chestnut Hill twp 9/3/1768-(?). ch Christopher, Elizabeth
    (Wey), Catherine, Magdalen, Margaret, Sophia, Henry. Adam Correll John
    Shneider, Ludwig Gawr W
    Christman 132 365 665
    Christy 109
    Clark 101 161 227 440 458 483
    Clasy 722
90 CLAUSS: John, Bethlehem twp yeoman. 13/12/1794-24/2/1796. Elizabeth w. ch
    George, Henry X, Philip, John, Abraham, Danielm Mary; mens lds of Philip
    Clouss, James Bingham, Michael Kochler. co-X Thomas Hartman. Thomas
    Hartman, Samuel *Coleman, Michael Koehler W
    Clauss 91 223 470 599
91 CLAWELL: George, Plainfield twp yeoman 25/5/91-3/6/1793 Anna-Maria w. ch
    Jacob X, Elizabeth, (w of George Claus), John, Daniel, George X, Joseph,
    Francis, Catherine, Salome, Christian, Abraham, William Henry, Melchior
    Christ and Joachim Wigman W
    Clegg 46
    Cleiss 263
    Clendinin 401 402
    Cleppinger 25
    Clewell 91 104 345 381 622 682 700 702 718 765
    Clippinger 301
    Cllick (?) 206
    Closs 307
    Clouss 402
92 CLOWSE: John George, Bethlehem twp farmer 5/2/1763-28/2/1763 Christina w X.
    ch mens George, minor, and other ch. William Edmonds of Bethlehem co-X.
    Ephriam Colvil, Andreas Folk W
    Clydie 234
93 CLYDE: Michael, Allen twp farmer 15/11/1785-23/4/1795 Bridget w X. mens "2
    eldest ds heirs Anna's and Mary's and 2 s ons John and James X
    three other d Margaret, Lettice and Elizabeth" John Hays and John Ralston W
    Clymer 24 411 526
    Clyne 360
94 CODER(Koder): Conrad, Plainfield twp yeoman. 2/4/1793-21/5/1793. Anna-Mary
    w. ch. Conrad X, Catherine-Elizabeth, Martin-Conrad, Agatha (w of Jacob
    Juncker)* (*read Martin-Conrad) Peter Obershimer, Peter Bender, J. Juncker W
    Cole 96 720
    Coleman 90
    Colver 70 345 386 683
    Colvil 92
    Coningham 44 443

95 CONNELEY: Thomas, Mt. Bethel twp 10/9/1793-3/2/1794 Hannah, w X. and s
   William X. mens 4 ch John (minor), Thomas, Hannah and William. Colonel
   Jos Martin of Mt. Bethel co-X. William Connelly, James Hess and James
   Culbreath W
   Conrad 338
   Cook 59
   Cooper 290
   Coordsen 620
   Correll 57 89 259 459 594 624 665 686
   Correy 326
   Corroy 141
96 CORTRIGHT: *Henry: "Dillaware twp" 27/3/1787-20/4/1787 gds Cornelius c.
   s Benjamin. decd. X. and Manuel Hover X. mens "gds Henry Corthright s of eldest
   s Cornelius, decd.: s Damiel and his s Benjamin: gds John s of Benjamin:
   gds William s of William: Ennis Cortright: gds Anthony s of Abraham
   Cortright decdM gds Daniel Van der Mark, s of my dau Jeane Corthright
   Vandermark. gds Jonathan Hover s of my dau Cornelia C. Hover; poor s
   William Ennis Cortright; gddau Sarah Cortright, dau of my s Benjamin: gddau
   Jeane Hover d of my dau Cornelia Hover" Ezekiel Schoonover, Moses Cole and
   Thomas Landon W
97 CORTRIGHT: Johannes, Delaware twp 8/2/1772-6/6/1772. mens bros William-Enner,
   Abraham and Benjamin Cortright. Janitz Cortright Hover; sis Yanice C (w of
   Johannes Vandermark). Manuel Gonsales X. Andreas Phenix, Abraham Lane,
   Henry Decker W
   Cortright 719
   Cosan 732
   Cougelton 399

98 COURTRIGHT: *Daniel, Delaware twp farmer 7/1/1788-17/6/1788. Renan(?)w. ch
   Levi, Gideon, David, Joseph, Hester (Vandermark), Yonuhe(?) (Decker), Caty
   (Decker), Daniel, Cornelius, Levi and Gideon XX. Guisbert Sutfin and
   Johannes *Decker W
   Courthright 678
   Covert 442
99 COYL: *Martha, wid of John, L. Smithfield twp 29/5/1795-10/4/1799 mens David
   Williams. John Fish X. James Johnston, Daniel Williams W
100 CRAFFORD: *Rebecca w of John, decd. 9/5/1778-15/5/1778. "her other ch Rebeca,
   Mary, Rachael" Elijah s X. robt. Moody X. gds John Clark. John Ihrie, Anthony
   and Thos Moore W
101 CRAFFORD: *John, weaver. 2/5/1778-15/5/1778 Elijah s X. and Robert Moody X.
   Rebecca w ch Martha, Susanna, Abigail, John, Edmund, Rebecca, Mary, Rachael,
   George. Anthony Moore, John Ihrie, Thomas Moore W
102 CRAIG: *Thomas, senior Allen twp 25/11/1772-6/1/1779. mens cousin Thomas Craig
   s of my bro Daniel: gds William Craig: William Logan of Phila. dil Elisabeth
   Craig; s William's ch Charles, William, Mary, Sarah, Margaret, Elizabeth, Ann
   and Hugh. bil Richard Walker, Esq X. Arthur Lattimore X. John Ralston X Wm
   Carruthers, Robt Lattimore, Thos Herron W
   Craig 9 74 370 403 411 433 567
   Crane 117 767
   Crantz 507
   Creutz 69 780
   Cruickshank 398

103 CRUMBACH: Conrad: innholder. 20/1/1781-8/2/81 Catharina w. ch Christina, Eve (w of Andrew Rub), George-Henry X, Conrad, Margared. Geo.Groff co-X. Peter Rhoads, Lorentz Hauck, and Mathias Ringel W
Cunow 127
Cuntramen 291
Custer 537
Cuthright 720
Babler 664
Daly 398

104 DANCKE: Frederick. 12/4/1793-2/3/1793. Ann-Mary w and iss male and female. John Youngsberg X, Jacob Christ X. Joseph Otto, Nathaniel Clewell and Gottfried Belling W

105 DANCKEL: *John, Macungie twp 16/8/1777-22/8/1778. Janincka w X. ch Peter (minor), Jacob, and others. Christian Miller X, Henry Equer X Michael Diehl, Christian Toegli W
Danckel 591
Daniel 511
Danielson 231

106 DANNER: Dietrich, Macungie twp yeoman 2/11/92-27/11/1792 Magdalena w. 4 ch Vatharina, Elizabeth, Magdalena, John (under 15 years) mens lds of George Shafer, Elias Weaver X and Henry Hrobbenberger X. Johann-Jacob Stefan and Peter Kuhn W

107 DANNY: *John Philip, Up Milford twp shoemaker 24/12/1763-24/1/1764 Mary-Margaret X. ch Simon Peter, Catharina, Elizabeth and John Philip. Peter Hertel co-X. John-Adam Reichenbscher, Benjamin Meyer, Abraham Meyer, Jacob Shuffer and Jacob Reiber W
Dauber 377
Dauff 757

108 DAVID: Mary, Plainfield twp widow. 12/3/1770-23/2/1774. mens d Elizabeth Jones of Virginia (iss William Cherrick, Mary, Margaret)M gds George David and Ephriam David: son's wf Mary Davies (iss). "Only son George-David" X mens Lewis David. Walter Miller, Margaret Rainsey and William Edmonds W
Davidson 499
Dawson 499
Deal 113

109 DEALING: John, Nazareth 9/8/1785-25/10/1785. Mary Magdalena w X and guar. mens ld in Northumberland: sold ld 4/2/1784 to Jacob Rouchemberger: purchased ld of Abraham Sorver; lds in Camden, Gloucester Co. N.J. mens his s Jacob and John Andrew. bil Sebastian Graff of Lancaster X. Joseph Demuth and William-Edmonds W
Dealing 162 606
Dech 37 536

110 DECKER: Jacob, Delaware twp yeoman 29/9/1777-2/8/1795. Margaret w X. ch Beaver (eldest s), Magdalena, Maria, Abraham, and "youngest s, unnamed" Ezekiel *Decker X W, Elias *Decker, X W, and Joseph Chestnor W

111 DECKER: Brewer, Delaware twp 1/10/1777-23/4/1777 Morratie w. ch Hendrine (eldest s) Johannis X, Elisha X, Jacob X, Yanatie (w of Lourence Decker), Leah (decd and iss). Gilbert Van Gorden, Lodowick Hower and Yost Chestnor W

112 DECKER: Benjamin Up Smithfield 10/9/1779-27/10/1779. mens Yonuhu d (w of Elias Decker); "except chest, bequeathed to his wif's s Sam-"uel" Johannes Vanetten d of Yonuhe's s Benjamin Decker, minor. "to. his s Daniel Decker's ch Lenah, Benjamin and Leah". "his s Samuel Decker X and Aurt Van Dike X. Guisbert Sutfin and Aurt Dike W

-12-

Decker 97 98
Deemer 34
113 DEETER: *Hans William, Lehigh twp yeoman. 10/12/1783-29/5/1790. Elizabet
    w. ch William (youngest s), Adam (eldest s) John, ? (w of John Lum) Hannah
    (w of George Deal), Julian (w of Conrad Meyer), Susanna (w of Lenard Beck),
    Elizabeth. bil Enoch Bear X and nephew John Deeter X George Palmer W
Deiber 361 496 671
Deichman 534 569
Delb 691
114 DELFS: Detlif: C. (?)-10/8/1795. John-Frederick Freuauff and John-Frederick
    Moehring W
Delfs 445 636
115 DELONG: *Abraham, Lynntsp 21/12/1755-22/9/1756 Cathron w. Peter s. Mathias
    Yooran X and Geo. Brinen X both of Lynn. John Everitt and Hannes Brown W
Delp 568
Demuth 109 224 247 302 351 696 718
116 DENEKE: Jeremias, Bethlehem, (?)-23/2/1796. mens Elizabeth: Christian-
    Frederick s. John Schropp, John Hasse W
Dencke 231
Dengler 372
117 DENMARK: *Christopher 5/6/1757-21/11/1757 "being greeviously shotten by the
    Indians, but "of perfect mind and memory" Leah w X. Dirck Van Vliet, William
    Smith and Jacob *Swartswood W. Amos Crane W (His wf lived 16 days after her
    husband's death and appointed William Smith, Domingo Gonsales her X on oath of
    Margaret Swartswood.
118 DEENMART: John Christophal, Up Smithfield twp 6/11/1755-(?) Christeena-
    Elisabeth w X. ch Christopher, Cathrine, Margreda, Dorothy, Helen iss.
    Emanuel Gonsales co-X. Christopher Denmark and Manuel Gonsales W
Denmark 720
Deobold 729
119 DEPUE: James "nuncupative will" L. Mt Bethel 10/10/1791-10/10/1791 mens his w
    Sarah: his fath, Benjamin Depue Esq; his bros Moses, Abraham and John.
Depue 3 425 463 491 652 663 668 720 731 735
Derhon 231
Dermott 138
120 DERR: John, Up Milford twp yeoman, 19/5/1794-5/9/1796 Magdalene w ch John X,
    Jacob, Elizabeth (w of George Horlacher jr had iss) and "others". Michael
    Fackenthall co-X. Thomas Linder and George Stahl W
Derr 317 568 755
Dersum 485
Desh 212
121 DESHLER: Appolonia Sept 1781: Renunciation of X ship of Adam Deshler's will
    (q v) Yost Fullert amd Juliana *Schriber W. (see Eyerman's Genealogical
    Studies)
122 DESHLER: Adam Whitehall twp yeoman. 22/1/1772-20/9/1781. Appolonia w X. ch
    David X, Peter, Adam, Eva-Catherina (w of Peter Burghalter), Juliana (w of
    George Schriber), Barbara (w of Philip Boehm), Catharina (w of Peter Kearn),
    J. Okely, Just Janson W. (see Eyerman's Genealogical Studies)
123 DESHLER: David, Salidbury twp. 2/11/1796-31/12/1796. Susannah w X. ch John-
    Adam (eldest s), George, David, Catherine (w of Charles Deshler), Barbara
    (w of John Wagner), Susannah (w of Fredk Peissel), Elizabeth (w of Jacob
    Meekly), Mary, Sarah. mens his bro °eter; lds in Allen twp. George Shrieber
    and George Jacob Newhard both of Allen twp X. John Hasse, Felix Grieseman
    and Jacob Warren W.

124 DESHLER: Adam, Whitehall twp yeoman 2/5/1789-8/3/1790 Maria-Catherine w. ch
David, under w 21 yrs- and others, bro David Deshler and George Schryber
X. Peter Burkhalter, Jacob Strein and Stephen Balliet W.

125 DESHLERN: Peter senio, Allen twp. (?)-19/11/1800 ch Peter, Jacob, David,
Sara, Susanna, mens lds of Henry Eple, Robert Hess and Christian Hagenbuch.
Jacob Schreiber, Michael Bieber, and s Peter X. Henry Epple, J Strein W
Deshler 20 54 273 739 (and Eyerman Gen. Studies)

126 DETER: John senior, Moorestown. 12/5/1772-4/6/1773. Elizabeth w. ch John X
and 8 others. J-Egidius Hecker, Adam Mersch, Ch. Laffer w

127 DETMERS: Ferdinand: Bethlehem gent. 28/2/1797-1/10/1801 Christina-Dorothea
w X. mens friend John-Christian Reich; the wid of Conrad Detmers of
Heidersheim, Saxony: ch of his bil Andreas-Ludwig Morhart "missionary
in Labrador"; Hans-Ch von Schweinitz. in codicil mens John Gebhard Cunow
X and Anton Smith X, Abraham Levering and David Weinland W
Detmurs 22 413
Detweiler 394
Devore 667
Dewalt 729

128 DEYLIE: Frederick, ( )/1790-9/10/1790. Henry Rentzheimer X. Daniel Diehl
X. John Resmus of Salisbury X
Dick 411

129 DICKENSHIED: John, Up Milford twp saddler 11/8/1800-19/11/1800 Mary w X. ch
Charles, Elizabeth, Mary, Jacob, mens ld of Conrad Meyer; fil Frederic Martin
X. Frederick Krammer and Wendel Wieant W

130 DEFENDERFER: John, Macungie twp yeoman 5/11/1780-14/2/1782 Magdalena w. ch
John (minor), Magdalena, Mary et al. Godfried Defenderfer X friend Jacob
Moor X. John Baer, Jacob Herman W

131 DIEFENDERFER: *Gertraut, wid of Alexander of Macungie 29/5/1777-22/12/1789
Godfried s X. and other ch. Jacob *Shmayer, Nicholas Klotz and Lewis Klotz W
Diefenderfer 27

132 DIEHL: Michael 21/11/1795-28/11/1796 John Diehl X. Jacob Rothanberger X David
Heimbach and George Christian (Christman) W

133 DIEHL: *Nicholas, Plainfield farmer 2/4/1800-1/5/1800 mens Elizabeth Rebsher
(housekeeper), Gottlich Schneider: Elizabeth Menzen: John Williams; Sarah
Bohannen d of Rebecca Schneider: John Rebsher given lds in L. Mt. Bethel.
Jacob Heller and James Hall X. Michael Smith and Sarah *Smith and Christian
*Shuck W
Diehl 105 128 132 174 447 643 690 801

134 DIEHL: Henry 26/3/1771-(?) had w and 4 ch incl Henry (eldest s), Fredk. Nagel
and Christian Miller X. and guar. George Kleppinger and John-Adam Hilterbrand W
Diemer 36 584
Dieter 454 644

135 DIETHARD: George-William Lehigh twp farmer 4/6/1774-12/10/1774. Magdalena w X.
and iss. mens Henry Strauss guar of s John. bil Joest Dreisbach co-X. Peter
Anthony, Henry Strauss W
Dietrich 425 449 667 701 702 757 763

136 DIETZ: George, L. Saucon yeoman 9/5/1758-7/11/1774. Anna-Maria w. sil Philip-
Henry Shull X Andrew Orstrom, David Owen, Corbelius Weygant and Peter Steiner W
Dietz 259

137 DILDINE: Andrew Up Mt Bethel yeoman 28/2/1793-;7/4/1793 Anna *Magdalene w X.
ch Sarah, Henry, Mary, Andrew, Daniel, Uatharine, Herman John and a ch unborn.
mens ld in Big Fishing Creek, Northumberland. s Henry and sil John Frutz X.
John Faume, John McCarter W

138 DILLDINE: Herman, Up Mt Bethel yeoman 3/11/88-8/5/1790 Margaret w X. ch Henry,
    Nancy, William. bro Andrew Dilldine X and bil Benjamin Goodwin X. John Faunce,
    Thos Aten Dav.BennetW
    Dildine 425 434
    DILLBAUER 716
    Dillon
139 DILLON: Neal, Allen twp 11/3/1761-18/3/1761 mens James Gray X: his mother
    Margaret; and sis. John Neale, Jno Tayler Saml Carruthers W
    Dingler 710
    Dingman 541
    Diper 140
140 DITTUS: Tobias (a baker) 29/12/1775-17/5/1779 mens Magdalene w. maid Suphia
    Fenchel: and sis Michael Diper X. bartel Hoover, Peter Rhoads and Gottlieb
    Boltzius W
    Dixey 205
141 DOBBIN: *Mary Allen-town 6/3/1762-17/6/1762 Alexander, Leonard (iss), Susanna,
    Jean (female), William, James, Elizabeth, bro William Boyd of London Grove,
    Chester Co. X Geo. Correy of New London, Chester Co X James Kerr, William
    Kerr W
142 DOFFERT: Adam Forks twp 7/12/1778-10/4/1779 "6 ch" but mens Jacob s, Eve and
    Mary dau. John and 4 youngest ch George, Susannah, Frederick, Philip minors.
    Jacob Weigant X Jacob Christ, William Edmonds W
143 DOLL: Casper, Plainfield 13/6/1792-20/3/1793 mens Johannes Doll. Fridrich Hahn
    and Jacob Peter W. John Young X. Lewis Stacher.
144 DOLL: Valentine, Salisbury 2/9/1758-24/10/58 Eve w. Nicholas eldest s iss male
    and female Barnld Stroup X, George Stout X. John Jennings and Henry Kocher W
    Doll 168 346 458 685 716
    Donart 354
    Donner 753
    Dormeyer 496
145 DORNBLESSER: Gottlieb (Thernblesser); Bethlehem twp yeoman 16/4/1780-23/1/1783
    mens his w (perhaps her second mar); ch John-Jost, John-Paul, Magdalena.
    Mary-Magdalena w X. ch Newman, Peter Shoemaker W
    Dornblesser 201
146 DORNY: *Daniel, Macungie, yeoman 15/1/1779-27/3/1780. Elizabeth w. ch John X,
    Daniel X, Henry X, Philip, AnnaKmaria, Eve, Barbara, Catherina, Magdalena,
    Peter, Adam. Conrad Brey and Peter Miller W
147 DORSCHIMAER: *Manuel, Chestnut Hill twp (?)-15/8/1798 Christina w X. John George
    X Henry and John George W
148 DOUGLAS: *Deborah, Neward, N.J. 15/2/1786-28/2/1786 "usual Ogton of Newark"
    mens gds John Sands: gddau Nancy Sands; Rev John Chapman, "Presbyterian
    minister near Newark": Paul Greer of Gnaudenhutten, Penn twp Northampton
    David and Ezra Warner W. "s Christian Miller# Sands enters cave at 23/2/1786,
    and hearing held 3/4/86 before Peter Rhoads and Robert J. Levers Esqrs Justices
    and John Arndt Esqr Register, at which time it was decided that the textatrix
    was of unsound mind, and letters of administration were granted to son"
149 DRAKE: Samuel, L. Smithfield 27/6/1783-16/4/1789. Sarah w X. ch Robert (youngest
    s) Thomas X, Elijah X, Joseph, Levy, Robert, Sarah, Susannah (w of Jos.
    Vanvleet), Elizabeth (w of Edward Evans), Phebe, Ruth, Hannah, Eleanor (w of
    James Horner, iss). gdch Samuel and signed James Drake, Jacob Stroud, Francis
    Smith and Samuel Handy W
    Drake 60
150 DREISBACH: Jost (?)-29/10/1794 John and Adam Dreisbach X. Gottlieb Andreas,
    J. Schaeffer W

Dreisbach 135 272 301 343 354 371 564 683 729
Dreyspring 713 793
Dressler 337
151 DRUCKENMILLER: Sebastian (?)-26/2/1795 Jacob Bortz and Frederick
    *Frederick W
Druckenmiller 279 649 715 745
Drum 37 205 564
152 DRUMM: Philip Moore twp yeoman (?)-22/11/1788 Jonakan w. ch Philip, Simon,
    John-Jost, Catharout (w of Henry Strousse), Elizabeth (w of Ph Swartz),
    Anna-Maria (w of Bartel Lawfer), Mary-Angle (w of Ludwig Bartlemew),
    Catarina (decd w of George Snyder), H. Bartgelus and George Palmer W)
Drumheller 194
Drunson 170
Dubler 572
Duffel 421
Dullford 520
Dulpenderfer 745
Dunham 420 533
Dunlap 269 22
Dunn 39 233 658
153 DURHAM: John Mt Bethel 29/4/1774-25/5/1774 Catharine w X. Robert Foreman X
    John Smith and Hugh Foresman W
Eacker 547
Ealer 82 175
154 EBENREITER: Michael 7/7/1790-2/5/1792. Margaret Ebenreiter X. Michael Huber W
155 EBERD: John, Plainfield 10/3/1776-(?) ch Philip X, Adam X, George X, Lisa-
    Barbara, Mary-Marfared, Mragrad. Lewis Stecher, Henry Hapel, and George
    Mombauer W
Eberhard 332 536
156 EBERT: Christian, Bethlehem, storekeeper. 12/4/1796-22/8/1799 Anna-Rosina w X.
    ch George-Fredk, and Elizabeth-Bening Ebert. sis in law, Elizabeth Youngman.
    Abraham Levering X. Franz Thomas and Joseph Horsfield W
Ebert 451 790
Eckel 474
157 ECKER: *George, Lehigh twp yeoman 5/11/1789-18/2/1800 Anna-Margaretha w. "all
    my ch" Philip s X, Jacob s X, Henry Biegely, William Kermer and Nicholas
    Anthony W
158 ECKERT: John, Williams twp yeoman 2/2/1789-18/(read 2/2/1787-(?). Mary-Eve
    w. ch John (elder s), Margareth, Abraham X, Batlhaser X. Adam Hartman W
Eckert 352 472
Edel 361
Edelman 271 641
159 EDINGER: Peter 18/8/1777-(?) 10 ch incl Conrad, the eldest, and William.
    Reinhart Edinger bro X, Melchior Edinger (Reinhart's s) X. Conrad Rosli and
    Paul Brodt W
160 EDINGER: Reinhard, L. Saucon, tailer 2/10/1779-22/12/1779 sons Meleker X,
    Abraham, Peter, Joseph Frey and Anthony Louhn W
161 EDELMAN: Jost, Plainfield 13/11/1767-15/4/1769 Anna Christina X. mens John
    Edelman and George sons of his bro John-George Edelman; Maria-Barbara
    and Margaret minors, 2 d of decd bro Maria-Magdalena, "another of his bros ch"
    Thomas Clark jr W
Edmiston 442

162 EDMONDS: William, Nazareth. (75 yrs age) 4/8/1782-16/9/1786 mens eldest
    d Margaret and her hus August Schlesser: Rev Nathaniel Seidel: Mary d,
    Judith, youngest d. gddau Mary Edmonds had bros and sis: s John and his
    eldest s. George Golkowsky. sil August Schlesser X. Mary X, Judith X&
    William Henry, John Dealing, Joseph Otto W
163 EDMUNDS: Judith, Nazareth 20/9/1796-11/10/96 mens Elizabeth Hopson: Philipina
    Enssin: bro John "and his ch" Jacob Christ X, Jacob Etterly, Elizabeth
    Rice W
    Edmonds 108 109 142 185 200 235 423 428 470 520 600 601 683 790 700 749 797
    Edwards 70
    Eggert 378 739 768
    Enger 105 316 529
    Ehrenhard 648
    Ehrenfried 409
    Ehrhard 167 292 467 648 778
164 EHRNHARD: Jacob, Salisbury 4/2/1760-27/2/1760 Barbara w. ch Catherine,
    Elisabeth, Anna-Maria John, Christina, Barbara, Susanna; George Kelin
    and Sebastian Knauss X, Peter Hoffman, Ludwig *Antres. J. Matthew Otto, J.
    Oakly, Peter Trexler W
    Ehwein 231
    Eisenhart 358
    Elliott 234
165 EMERICH: Jacob (?)-31/3/1797. Jacob Beck, John Adam EyerW
    Emerich.198
    Emmens 652
166 EMMENSTETTER: *Elizabeth wid of Conrad 4/12/94-4/2/1796 mens her mother Mary
    Beans; cous. Elizabeth Limbach;d of Fredk and Mary Limbach; s Joseph X.
    George Huber X. Joseph Gambold, Frederick Limbach of Hope Essex Co W
    Emrich 416 456
    Encke 562 741 747
167 ENGLE: Thomas, Lowhill. 18/4/1777-16/5/1777 Elisabeth w. ch Casper, Adam,
    George, Magdalena, Mary, Conrad, Elisabeth, (some minors). friend George
    Ehrnhart, Leter Shoemaker, George Christian Reiss W
    Engle 276
    Engleman 210 656 792
168 ENGLER: Adam, Plainfield 29/3/1763-7/6/1763 Aplon w and 6 ch. James Sorber,
    Casper Doll W
    Engler 353 609 667
    Enssin 163
169 ENTRES: Michael, Up Milford 17/2/1782-18/4/82 Ann-Elizabeth w. mens John Machlin,
    "s now with his parents, moved to Pittsburgh, minor" Mary and Michael Hains,
    decd step bros ch; Elizabeth Stahl d of Jacob Stahl: Michael s of Jacob
    Stahl: bro Daniel Entres, "in high Germany, Kyrbrag" step bro Jacob Hains:
    step bro Fredk Hains of Macungie, decd haf iss (d Johannah Hains) Jacob Stahl
    X, George Seider X Caveat entered 21/3/1783 by widow: present at hearing:
    Robert Leversm Fredk Limbach, Abraham Berlin, John Arndt. W to will Adam
    Reinhart, Gabriel Robameister, Fredk Limbach
    Eple 125
    Eprecht 182
170 ERB: Casper, widower 29/4/1788-1/9/1788 ch Jacob (Moore twp eldest s), Laurence,
    Margaret (w of Philip Drunson), Elizabeth (w of David Blackley), Michael;
    cous, Elizabeth Hog. mens lds of Nicholas Miltenberger, Jim Ritters, Fredk
    Beck, Jim Grove, Gep Jacoby, Peter Rundie, Geo Palmer, Fredk Gutekunst. bil

170 EBB:
     Peter Seip X. George Palmer, Conrad Kreiter W
     Erbach 561
171 ERB: (VAN): Adam, Bethlehem, Breechesmaker 23/2/1794-23/2/1796 Patience
     w X. 3 s Nathaniel, Joseph, John. Anthony Smith co-X. Eberhard Freitag,
     John Hasse W
172 ERDMAN: *Andrew, Up Saucon, yeoman 11/3/1795-10/4/1795 ch Jacob X, Catherine
     (w of Jacob Bernhart), George, Yost, Andrew, Margaret (w of George Sober),
     John, Abraham, Elizabeth, (w of Geo Frantz), Sibylla (w of Henry Bitz).
     John Waltman, Jacob Rumfield, Henry Kooken W
     Ernst 85 368 727
     Erdman 76 444 754
173 ERNST: Michael, L. Saucon, weaver 21/6/1792-21/12/1792 mens s Michael X,
     dau Elizabeth (w of George Kuntsman) iss Daniel, Michael, Henry and Christina
     Kuntsman. Frederick Werner, Philip Kuntsman W
     Esch 658
174 ESCHBACH: Christopher, Salisbury, joiner. 31/3/1795-10/1/1797 Catherine w X.
     ch Elizabeth (w of Henry Snider), George, John-Adam, Mathias, William, David,
     Susannah, Anna-Marie. mens ld of Henry Borger. Michael Weber of Saucon X
     and guar. Daniel Diehl guar. John Hasse and Peter Weber W
     Eschbach 81
     Eschelman 5
     Esh 258
     Esterlein 701
     Ettwein 8 222 235 302 630 713 730 740
     Everett 26 115 197 287 288 498 672
175 EVERHARD: *Arnold, Easton, weaver 1/2/1782-18/3/1782 Margaret w X and 7 ch.
     Peter Ealer, Philip Helick, Conrad Ihrig W
176 EVERITT: Asa, Up Mt Bethel twp yeoman 18/8/94-11/11/1794 Margaret w. ch Sarah,
     Elisha X, Mary, William, Joseph, Susannah, John, James; Moses Everitt of Up
     Mt Bethel co-X. Edward Hunt of Knowlton twp Sussex Co N.J. co-X John J.
     Hendrix, Thomas Beer W
     Everitt 86 349 382
     Evans 149 200 292 457
     Eyer 165 327 618
177 EYERLY: Jacob, the elder, Nazareth, yeoman 1/12/1790-7/10/1800 Christina w. ch
     Jacob X, Elisabeth (w of Owen Rice), Christina (w of Henry Beck). Jacob Christ
     co-X. William Henry and Jaochim Witman W
178 EYERLY: Jacob, Nazareth 3/5/1800-(?) Anna-Maria w. ch Elizabeth, Jacob, Anna-
     Maria, John, Susanna, Theodora. mens his mother: sisinlaw Elizabeth Penkerton:
     lds in N.J. in Plainfield and Moore twps. mill and extate called Friedensthal.
     Joseph Shweishoupt and Abraham Levering X and guar. Nicholas Kreamer X.
     Thomas Hartman, John Christ and Jacob Boerstler W
     Eyerly 163 226 308 339 365 590 599 600 702
     Eyerman 83 121 122 123 124 125 275 276 326 456 739
     Fackenthall 120
     Fahlstick 453
     Falhever 533
     Faneberg 601
     Farten 431
     Fatzinger 548 760
     Faume 137
     Faunce 138 393 763

Fauner 392

Fausele 694

Feer 435

Feedter 662

179 FEGER: Michael, L Saucon twp 12/10/1769-26/10/1769 Anna-Barbara w. mens
    Valentine, youngest ch and Maria-Catrena. Melcher Knepley X Michael Heller
    and George Scheive W

180 FEHLER: Adam, L Saucon 8/8/1777-9/5/1777 Dorothy w and 10 ch. sil Michael
    Ketter. sil John Housman: Adam s. Valentine Opp X. George Rothrock X.
    Daniel Lawall, Jacob Koch, James Chapman W

Felix 211 773

Felker 209

181 FELL: Nicholas, Mt Bethel, yeoman 27/4/1784-26/7/1784 Margaret w X. mens ch
    Henry X, Mary Magdalin, Catreeny; Adolph Flory Ph. Schuck W

182 FELTER: *Johannes, Weissenberg twp 28/8/1759-13/11/1759 mens his w and ch
    Margrata Grundin, Mary Bowrin, Jacob Jentzer X. Rudolph Eprecht, Valentine
    Grambich, Thomas Bover W

Fenchel 140

Fenner 29 214

183 FENSTERMACHER: Barbara, Bethlehem 1/11/1782-17/12/1790 ch George X, Mary
    (present w of Mr. Lorentz Bagge of N. Car), Martin, Peter, Henry, gddau
    Charlotte (d of decd s Andrew) Tobias Boeckel W. Codicil 24/9/1783, declared
    that Mary died and left iss Jonathan, Gottlieb, John-Christian and Elizabeth
    Fakie. mens s George Leibert and William Boehler of Bethlehem

184 FENSTERMACHER: William (?)-28/12/1801 mens George and Wm. Fenstermacher X.
    Geo Horn, Martin Andrews W

Fenstermacher 366 371 372 251

185 FELTHAUSER: Henry "formerly of Schnectady but now in the Barony of Nazareth,
    cooper" 14/8/1783-14/8/1799. Beala w X. William Edmonds, John Youngsberg
    and Jacob Christ W

Fetter 156 462 575 662

Fetterhof 68

Figel 711

186 FILTZINGER: Andrew L. Saucon 8/7/1766-7/12/1767 Anna-Margaret w. mens Dorothea
    (w of John Henry Seitz of N. Car. iss). gds Andrew. X and sil Christopher
    Waggoner of L. Saucon X. Valentine Opp and Godgrevd Richter W

187 FINCH: Michael, Salisbury, weaver 28/7/1773-28/8/1773 mens Elizabeth w. ch
    Peter (eldest), Michael (minor) et al. George-Adam Blank, Christopher
    Hausel and Jacob Geisinger W (Forlast 2 read Adam Wieder and John Smith W)

Finck 605

Finley 44

Finney 533

188 FISH: John, L. Smithfield. 6/2/1798-9/7/1798. mens Margaret w, Joseph and
    "several ch" John Brown and John Broadhead Esq X both of whom declined and
    Dana Ihrish and Jacob Williams were apptd. admins. Michael Hausberg and
    Francis-Joseph Smith W

Fish 99 678

189 FISHER: Christian, Up Milford 1/9/1779-(?) Maria-Magdalena w. mens Christian,
    eldest X Elizabeth, Rosinay, Margerity, Jacob, John, Peter, Leonard and
    Anthony. moth-in-law Justina Gibbart: servant, Maria Grosch. John-Adam
    Schuler co-X. Jacob Hayl, Nich. Stecher W

190 FISHER: Thomas, Bethlehem, hatter 6/1/1784-(?) mens Agnes w and dau Anne-
Maria X and Susannah. Jacob Wiesinger co-X Transp by John Hassey
Fisher 213 432 517 737
191 FLACK: John 16/2/1760-11/3/1760 mens w living: d Catherine and Anne-Mary.
Casper Wetterholt. Philip Moser, Philip Wertman, Peter Heimbach
Fleckinger 273 523
Fluckinger 404
Fleming 282
Flexer 589
Flick 564 625 658
192 FLICKINGER: *Ulrich, Whitehall twp yeoman 6/7/1772-19/6/1792. ch Jacob X, Peter,
George. sil Henry Heffelfinger and John Reese. Philip Lambach and Jacob
Kohler W
193 FLORES: Michael, Up Milford. 13/2/1773-11/3/1773 ch Catherine (w of Martin
Ringle), Elizabeth, (w of George Sieder), Anna-Margaretha. Matthias HornX,
Jacob Wetzel X. George Welter, Peter Teiss and J. Weaver W
194 FLORY: *John. 2/4/1801-16/5/1801. Christina w. mens Ludwig s. Christina and
Ludwig Flory X John Drumheller W
Flory 181
Fly 492
195 FOERSTER: Christian, Nazareth, weaver. 15/5/1795-15/5/1795. mens "3 ch of
decd sister Frederick Seffel, Gottlieb Seffel in Neuwied and Hoffman in the
West Indies" friend Francis Seiffert: Christian Schweinitz; bro Gottlieb
Forester in Stettin: bro John-Christian Foerster of Gerpsdorf in Lusatia:
sis Elizabeth Teirichin: Nicholas Heber X. Francis Seiffert X. John Beatel
and Henry Miller W
196 FOGEL: John, senior, Macungle twp yeoman 2/2/82-30/6/1782 Margareth w. John,
X, Philip X, Henry Jacob, Magdalena, Catharina, Margareth. John Moor co-X.
Peter Trexler jr. Geo. Breinig W
Fogel 473 664
Fogelman 85
Foltz 46
Foresman 153 289
Forsyth 250
Fosselman 350
197 FOULK: *George, Lynn twp 7/2/1761-22/1/1762 Dorothy w X. John Enerett, John
Holder Sr. Henry Romich W
Foulk 268 498 527 593
198 FOX: Christophel Mt Bethel farmer 8/3/1780-1/5/1780 Mary w. mens 5 ch incl
Jacob and Joseph. Jacob Emerich X, Jacob Beck X Robert Richard, John-Martin
Kogel W
Fox 225
Fraess 764
199 FRANCK: George, Allen twp yeoman 19/10/1780-(?) Anna-Mary w. George s. George
Koock X. John Weber, John "Kock", George Kock W
200 FRANCK: Anna Maria, widow, Allen twp 21/5/1797-24/1/1798 mens Anna-Maria
Musselman: Catharine w of Geo. Spingler, jr., Barbara w of Lewis Hoffman:
Sally w of Adam Mensch: Sibila wid of Conrad Leisering, Catharine w of John
Koch; Margaret w of Evan Evans X: and George Franck. Abraham Mensch co-X
Leonard Miller and Evan Evans W
Frank 200 700 701 702

201 FRANTZ₊ Paul, L. Saucon twp 3/12/1763-13/10/1766 Mary w. ch Nicholas,
     Paul, Ludwig X, Susanna (Artman), Catarina (Slough), Madland (Dornblesser),
     Mary X (Hartzell), Barbury (Grove). Fredk Gwinner, Johannes Huber, Anna-
     Mar Huber W
     Frantz 172 372 712
202 FREDERICK: John George, Smithfield, weaver. 13/9/1766-1/8/1772 Anna-Margreta
     w X. mens bro George-Michael Frederick: sis Anna-Margreta: Melcher Stecher,
     Jno Lesher, William Edmonds W
203 FREDERICK: Anna Margaret, his wid. 17/12/1772-19/1/1774 mens bil Geo-Michael
     Frederick: sis Anna-Elizabeth Mower, Anna-Mary Mower, Mary-Catherine Mower,
     Anna-Osula Mower. friend Jno Handelong, Peter Lober, Jacob Stroud X,
     Abraham Miller X. George Minehar, Jacob Snell, David Miller W
     Frederick 69 151 343 645 696
204 FREEMAN: *Richard, L. Saucon twp 9/7/1784-2/8/84 Rebecca w. mens William s of
     Plainfield, Sarah d (w of Jonas Thomas), gds Freeman Thomas s of Sarah: gdch
     John and Isaac Oberly ch of d Rebecca: Mary d (w of John Schweitzer of Berks)
     s Isaac X, s Edward X. John Hassy, Christoph Gierd and John Shouk W
     Freitig 171 439 512 634
     Freuauff 114
     Freuss 470
     Frey 7 160 468
     Freyhube 211
205 FRIDERICH: John, Allen twp yeoman 25/4/1790-14/6/1792 Eve-Barbara w. ch Daniel,
     George, Susanna, Mary, Barbara, Elizabeth, Salome, John; Bernhard Arndt, guar-
     trustee. John Rohn X James Dixey, Jacob Balliet, George Drum and Frederick
     Herman W
     Fries 338
     Fritz 22
     Froli 242
     Fromelt 8 630
206 FRUTCHIE: Frederick, L. Saucon 20/1/1779-1/3/79 Ann-Maria w X. 8 ch (minors)
     incl Frederick X? and John X? (given plantation in Williams) William and
     Jacob. Anthony Lezgh jr. Christopher Click (?), Adam Hartman, John Ludwig W
     Frutshy 137
     Fuchs 620 621 787
207 FUHR: Leonard, Heidelberg twp 23/7/1776-(?) mens bro John Fuhr: "my gossip
     Leonhard Schnyder": 4 sis Chatarina Schnyder, Susanna Webr, Margareth Scholl
     and Mary Fuhr. Geo. Bloss X
     Fuhr 662
     Fuehrer 222 423
     Fullbucht 618
     Fuller 459
     Fullert 122 281
     Fulston 536
208 FUHR: Leonard, Heidelberg twp 22/4/1766-(?) mens Mary-Catharina (?) and ch.
     John Wassum and Henry Geiger W
209 FULTON: John, L. Smithfield yeoman 7/2/1795-12/3/1795 Mary w and her dau Mary
     mens his father and mother Samuel and Mary Fulton: bros Alexander, Samuel and
     Andru Fulton: sis Elinor Moreland (w of Andru Moreland):sis Mary Rogers (w
     of John Rogers): lds in L. Saucon. John Shaw, Esq X, John Huston X. George
     Fulton, Catharine Huston and Ernest Kern W
210 FUNCK: John, Up Milford, yeoman 5/10/1781-12/11/1781 Catharina w X. ch Catharina,
     Charlot, Susanna. bro Rudolph Funck co-x. Adam Engleman, Jacob Smith and
     Peter Haye W

211 FUNCK: John Nicholas, Christian Spring, Nazareth 5/8/1791-24/8/1795. mens
     bro John-George Funk of Neudorf near Lobenstein, in Vogtland: cous John
     Felix: Martin Freyhube: "George Remer of Carolina shall get nothing"
     Paul Miksch), George Golkowsky X, Philip-Jacob Hoocker and Nathaniel Weber W
     Funk 348
     Gackenbach 215 551
     Gaeff 81
     Gaentzwig 680
     Gainly 293
     Galbreath 95
     Galloway 443
     Gambold 29 166
     Garrison 231 302
     Garton 70
     Gaston 476 482 708
     Gaumar 222
212 GAUMER: *Dietrich: Macungle, yeoman 11/6/1794-12/11/1794 Mary-Elizabeth w.
     ch Mathias X, John-Adam X, Johnn Frederick, Jacob, Gertie, (w of Henry
     Mertzler), Elizabeth (w of Henry Shankweiler). Jacob and Philip Desh W
     Gawr 89
213 GEBHARD: Leonhard, Up Milford 22/11/1776-12/8/1777 Anna-Mary w. mens "2 ch"
     incl Leonard: lds of Conrad Zellerand, Adam Riveland. Christian Fisher X,
     Anthony Slaterony X. Killian Weiss and John Ord W
     Gebhart 189 776
214 GEESY: Jacob, L. Saucon weaver 9/5/1785-4/7/85 Barbara w X. ch Barbara, Jacob,
     John, Catherine, Andrew, Ann-Mary. mens gdch of d Ann-Barbara (w of Mathew
     Werber of N. Car) Andrew Giering co-X of Emaus. Adam Sneider, Felix Fenner W
     Gehman 695
215 GERRY: Adam 3/10/1793-16/11/1793. John Lidweiler X. George Reichert, John
     Gackenbach W
     Geiger 78 208 217 243 334 537 538 633 709 751 756 757
     Giese 462
216 GEISS: *Henry, Macungie, yeoman 15/11/1784-16/12/1784. mens s Johannes-Peter
     X, Maria-Susanna Gutekunst dau of my dau Anne-Catherine; John-Adam eldest s:
     Ragina d; John-Nicholas s; John-Peter s. John Mohr, Jacob Herman, Herman Mohr
     W
     Geiss 637
217 GEISSINGER: Daniel, senior, L. Saucon, yeoman 31/10/1800-4/4/1801. Elizabeth
     w. ch Daniel X, Henry, Philip, Mary, Barbara, John, Elizabeth, Abraham, Joseph
     bro Philip Geissinger and friend Daniel Beidelman co-X. Leonard Geiger, Philip
     Leith and John Weiss W
218 GEISSINGER: Samuel, Up Milford 6/7/1773-(?) Augenes w X. and ch. bro John
     Geissinger coK Henry Kooken, Martin Schaeffer and Johannes Schlicher W
     Geissinger 252 326 530 643 679 703 700
     Geist 627
219 GEORGE: John Conrad: (?)-18/8/1798 mens Henry and John George X
     George 379 417 648
     Geiberich 718
     Gerhardt 47 51
220 GERINGER: Adam (?)-22/11/1791. mens John Hasse, of Bethlehem and Michael
     Schortz
     Germanton 1
     Gerrhdorf 231

Gerstenberger 478

Gerster 351

Getz 665

221 GEYSEL: Nicholas, Lehigh twp 23/2/1777-22/4/77 Anna w X. and guar of s Jacob. Conrad Shyder, Joseph Beaty and John Henky W

Gibbert 248

Gibson 795

Gierd 204

Giering 214 364 368 577 746 767

222 GIESEN: *Barbara, wid of Jacob (?)-10/8/1795 mens Elizabeth, Jacob and Anna Thomin: Julianna Gammarin: Jacob Sanders; Margaretha-Catharina Lembke: Carl-Gottlieb Reichel: Hans-Christian von Schweinitz; Johannes Schropp: Johann- Ch. Reich: Maria and Christian Ettwein: Maria-Magdalena Kleist: Elizabeth Fuehrer; Magdalena Schneider: Maria Hering: Christian Boring: Johannes Schropp and Anton Schmidt X. Jno. Merch and Abraham Huebner W

Giesie 766

Giess 366

223 GIFFIN: Peter, Bethlehem twp yeoman 25/10/1791-11/11/1791 mens Mary Reser, wid of Jacob Reser; the ch of his bro Aaron Giffin: the ch of his sis Sarah Todd, "who is the wife of Benjamin Todd of N. Car": William Henry Lawall X, Leonhard Beidelman X. Susanna Townsend, Joseph Jones and Philip Clause W

Gift 396

Gilbert 572

Gill 365 356 746

Gillam 300

224 GIRSCH: *Christian, Nazareth, carpenter. 5/6/1797-16/8/1797. Elizabeth w X. ch Elizabeth, Christina, Rosina, Joseph; Melchoir Christ guar of Joseph. Joseph Schweishaupt cp-X. Melchoir Christ, Joseph Demuth W

Giss 285

Glass 308

Gocken 263

Godfrey 339

225 GOEBEL: John, Salisbury, weaver 11/7/1785-9/5/1791 Sabina w X. sons Frederick, John, Valentine, Nicholas (all with iss). George-Adam Blank of Salisbury X. Nicholas Fox, John Horn and Peter Rhoads W

226 GOLD: *George Nazareth. 4/7/1792-19/9/1792 Anna-Maria w. ch David, George, Anna-Maria, Rosina, Dorothea. Jacob Eyerly jr X Joseph Levering Esq and Joachim Wigman W

Gold 23

Golkowsky 55 161 211 235 444 445 481 549 588 596 636 682 776

227 GONSALES: Manuel, Delaware twp 28/2/1789-20/3/1789 Yanaky w. ch mens Samuel X (minor), Leanah (Oberfields), Catharina, Sarah, Elizabeth, mens "was a captive in Canada" mens gdch Manuel, Jean and Margaret dau of decd s Manuel; gdch Manuel, Benjamin, Rebekah, Martin, Elizabeth, Mary and Leanah Oberfields. Peter Quick X Benjamin Brintz X, Jacob Woolf X, John Turner X. William *Smith, John Clark, Robert Lockeby W

Gonsales 616 720 97 117 118

228 GOOD: George. 25/11/1769-(?) Elizabeth w. ch Daniel (mar), George, Felix; George Belman and George Knauss W

Good 270

Goodwin 86 138 434

Gor 295

Gordon 6 111 733

229 GOUGH: Elizabeth: "Exemplification" 5/6/1762 mens John, Archbishop of
    Canterbury: John Winchester of Nethersole: George Langdale of St. Clement
    Danes: Mrs A. Breecton of Borras Co. Danbig, wid. (relates to Penna Lands)
    **1 Register's office 7/1/1786 (see 532)
    Gough 532
230 GOWER: Nicholas, Hamilton twp 21/3/1786-2/8/90 Mary-Elizabeth w. ch George X,
    Simon, Ludwig, Elizabeth, Susanna, Catherine, Michael, Peter France coX.
    Jacob Steelsmith, John Laurence and Bartel Scheilli W
***1 (see 229) also mens Benjamin Wood of the Parish of St Ann, Soho)
231 GRAEFF: Mathias. 31/1/1779-6/7/1779. mens Margareth (2500 pounds) M bros
    John, Jacob, George, Peter: sis Catherine Thomas: Elizabeth, George,
    Christina, ch of his sis Christina Sutton: John George, Henry, Margareth ch
    of George Moore: Nathaniel Seidel, John Ehwein and Christian von Schweinitz
    in trust for United Brethern and for Widows House: Susanna von Gerrhdorf and
    and Elizabeth von Seidlitz (single womens house) Andreas Basse and John Bonn
    (single men's house) Mathias Hehl, Adam Grube (Brethern Soc. Litiz): John
    Hopron, Henry de Hoff (united Brethern at Lancaster); John Elwein, Jeremias
    Dencke (Boys School); John Elwein, Timothy Horsfield; Paul Minster: Otto C.
    Krogstrop: Geo. Mixdorf; Rudolph Strachly; Michael Haberland; Nicholas Gar-
    rison: Anton Schmidt: Daniel Neighbert: George Bietschman: George Green:
    Samuel More: widow Derhon: Francis Thomas: bro Jacob Graeff X, Adam Richard
    X, Ephriam Colver, Peter Danielson and Thomas Bartow jr W. also mens Peter
    Danielson, hatter: sis Catharine Thomas (Estate valued at 9000 to 10,000 pounds)
    Graff 72 109 330 373 467 511
    Grame 325
    Gramer 774
    Granlich 182
    Gramus 715
    Grasya 310
232 GRATER: Daniel, Up Milford 30/10/1801-9/11/1801 Barbara w X. mens Jacob s of
    Henry Pitz: bros Jacob, David, John and Christian Grater: sis Elizabeth,
    Esther, Anna, Mary and Margaret. Andrew Andreas co-X Nicholas Hittel, John
    Shimer W
    Gray 59 87 139 340 723
    Green 67 231 237 323 763
    Greer 148 683
233 GREGG: *Margaret, Allen twp 26/12/1799-28/4/01 gddau Elizabeth and Ann McHenry:
    gds Francis and Mathew McHenry: lds of James Dun: John McNair and James
    Ralston X. John Weaver, Christian Hagenbuch W
234 GREGG: *Robert, Allentown, yeoman 16/12/1755-22/3/1756 Margaret w X. ch Robert,
    Margret, mens lds of John Gregg of Middletown, Bucks (read lds of John Elliott
    etc) mens John Gregg of Middletown Bucks co-X. Thomas Boyd, George Sharpe W.
    mens George Clydie, John Rhoads
    Gregg 795
235 GREITER: Gottfried, Bethlehem twp 12/4/1769-19/4/1769 mens bros Christian,
    Tobias and Geo. bil John-Nicholas Huber. Mr John Arbo X. Mr John Bon, steward
    of Christianbrun X, John Etwein, Pres of Genl. Deacons, Bethlehem
    Gresemer 374
    Gress 607 721
236 GRESSEL: Jacob, Heidelberg twp 30/9/1771-10/3/1774 "Our help is in the Lord,
    who made the Heavens and Earth: Amen" Ann-Mary w X. ch John-Jacob (eldest),
    Bernhart (youngest) et al. bil Bernhart Neff of Heidelberg co-X

Gretz 611
Grieseman 123
237 GRIM: Conrad, Weissenberg twp 18/3/1763-13/8/63 Elizabet w X. ch Diewald,
George, Jacob, Henry, Mary, Catarina, Magdalena, Susanna, Elisabeth, Jacob
Green and Henry Shaffer W
238 GRIM: Gitty, Macungie. 23/1/1760-1/10/1761. mens Jacob, Henry, Catharina,
Elisabeth, Margaretta. Frantz Roht s of my dau. Nicholas Hermany and Abr.
Brauss W
Grim 246 299 358
239 GRIESEMER: John, Whitehall, yeoman "Nuncupative Will" 7/10/1789-26/10/1789
George Herman X and Jacob Smith X. both of Up Milford
Grob 418
Groff 103 278
240 GROSS: Christian, senior, L. Saucon, yeoman 9/7/1793-5/11/1793 Mary w. ch
Daniel, Christian, Mathias, Urich, John, Magdalena (w of Charles Rentzheimer
of L. Sau), and Catharina. mens gds John Gross s of s Christian, minor:
lds of Daniel Beidelman. Christopher Wagner and Charles Rentzheimer of L.
Sau W. Jno Wagner, C Scheen
241 GROSS: Jacob, L. Saucon yeoman 12/5/1791-12/2/1792. Magdalena w. ch Susanna,
Sary, Philip, Jacob, Frederick X, Mathias, Conrad, John X, Margaret. John
Beyer guar mens lds of John Currie, Tobias Lerch. John Beyl and John Beyer W
242 GROSS: Philip, Germantown 19/3/1770-(?) mens Magdalena w. George-Daniel and
Mafdalena Gross: bro Jacob Gross X and Valentine Opp X both of L. Sau. Geo
Lesh, Leonart Freli, Ch. Gress W
Gross 496
Grossch 189
Groten 761
Grothouse 526 529 679
Grotz 475 550 673
Grove 170 201 324 325
Grube 231
Grundin 182
243 GRUENEWALD: Michael 20/7/1784-2/8/1784 Ludwig Stein and Henry Geiger W
244 GRUENEWALD: Ann Elizabeth (?)-18/10/1791 mens George Gruenewald, Ph Benninghoff,
Adam Miller W
Gruenewald 538
Grut 4
Gruver 472
Gutekunst 170 216 784
Guth 270 700
Gwinner 28 201 277 326
245 HAAS: John, L. Saucon, yeoman. 6/12/1783-21/5/1784 Catherine w X. 9 ch John,
Conrad, Jacob, Barbara (w of Adam Weber), Catherine, Anna-Catharine (w of
Michael Lawald), Dinah, Margareth, Elizabeth; mens lds of Christopher Heller
in Upper Swamp; Conrad s of Mary Heller (d of Ludwig Heller). John Haas
co-X. Wilhelm Boehler, John Haas, Just Johnson W
HAAS 354 573 726
246 HAASE: Peter, senior, Macungie 24/3/1777-(?) Catharina w ch John, Jacob,
Henry, John-George Elizabet (w of Jost Schaeffer, had 222 acres in Torky,
Foot twp Bedford Co), Maria (w of Jacob Scheidt), Salome; Jacob Grim, Adam
Brauss W
247 HABBACHER: *George, Moore twp cooper 18/4/1782-28/7/1783 Ana-Elizabeth w X and
gusr of his young ch. John Risburg, Chrestoph Demurh W

248 HABBES: Michael, senior, Penn twp 5/3/1783-21/3/1787 (intestate) Geo
     Gibbert, Geo Ziegler W
     Habbler 349
     Habbis 637
     Haberland 231
     Haff 637 726
     Haffey 305
249 HAFNER: Magdalena, Bethlehem (?)-26/6/1787 mens Margaretha Catharina Lemke of
     Bethlehem: Rosina Kremser; Maria Loph: Johannes Schopp X. Maria C Lembke
     and Catharine-Elisabeth Lewis W
250 HAGEL: Peter, Hamilton, blacksmith 2/1/1797-27/1/1797 Eve w. mens father
     Peter Hagel: bro Henry Hagel: sis Hannah (w of Valentine Makes), Ann
     (w of Caleb Forsyth), Catherine Hagel. friends Nicholas and John Heller.
     Jno Shaw, Ricd Shaw W
     Hagel 155
     Hagenbuch 72 125 233 603
     Hager 11
     Hahn 1 20 143 259 364 767
     Hain 748
     Hains 169
     Haintz 335
251 HAINY: *Philip, Moore twp yeoman 31/5/1782-16/3/1790 Anna-Maria w. ch Christian
     et al& George Rese of Allen X. Jno Fenstermacher, W& Kromer W
252 HALL: Philip, Up Saucon, yeoman 18/1/1773-24/2/1773 Ester w and George s (minor)
     and 4 dau. John Geissinger X. Henry Kooken and Geo Sawitz W
     Hall 74 133 395 529 549 610
253 HALLER: Anna (?)-4/6/1798. Adam Miller and Jacob Wannemacher W
254 HALLER: Henry, Gnadenthal 4/4/1788-6/5/1788 mens Elizabeth dau of (w of Peter
     Muecke): dau Anna-Catharine: dau Charlotta (w of Jacob Bulisher); dau
     Elizabeth (iss)N Michael Moehring: John Shropp: Henry Blum: Gottfried
     Belling: John Youngsberg of Nazareth X. William Henry Esq and Christian-
     Frederick Steinman W
     Hamman 270 705
     Handelong 203
255 HANDWERCK: John (?)-3/8/1789 Peter Kohler Esq. and Jacob Stoeckel W
256 HANDWERCK: John, Heidelberg twp 9/12/1785-(?) Anna-Maria w. ss John, Nicholas,
     Peter Kohler and Jacob Stoeckel W
     Handwerck 406
     Hanke 588
257 HANNA: Robert, L. Smithfield 5/5/1777-5/7/1777 mens his w. s Benjamin. gdss
     John Sealy, Robert Hanna s of Robert: gddau Elinor Sealy. T. Jayne X
     Hantz 666
258 HAPPEL: *Nicholas, Chestnuthill twp 6/10/1798-24/6/1799 John Serfass Esq and
     William Meyer X. Henry Bornman, Nicholas Esh, Henry Happel W
259 HAPPEL: *Henry, Plainfield, yeoman 21/4/1800-9/2/1801 Catharine w. ch Casper,
     George, Christian, Margaret (w of Wm Heidman), Catharine (w of Jacob Hofmer),
     Elizabeth (w of Abraham Dietz), Barbara (w of Henry Bartholomew), Sophy. s
     George X and Henry Bartholomew X. Michael Musselman, Frederick Hahn and
     Peter *Correll W
     Happel 718
     Hardy 149
     Harding 22

Harmony 576
Harpe 201
260 HARTLIL: George (untranslatable)
261 HARTMAN: John, Lowhill and Heydelberg twps. 13/5/1777-3/6/1777 ch Henry,
    Peter, Jacob, Christian, John, Mary. Eve-Mary his w. mens William Meyer's
    place in Lowhill and Heidelberg twps. Christian Miller and Christian Reiss W
    Hartman 28 90 158 178 201 206 232 283 295 298 366 415 423 518 645 783
    Hartung 714
262 HARTZELL: George, L. Saucon 31/3/1785-25/3/1789 Mary-Magdalena w. ch Henry,
    Mary, Margaret, Catharina (decd had iss), Soloman. mens "my wife's ch Adam
    and Magdalena Schmetzer" John Rothrock X. John Beyl, Philip Boehm, Isaac
    Shimer W
    Hartzell 201 292 397 434 549
263 HASHAW: Abraham, Williams twp. 4/11/1755-(?) mens his bro Henry: bro
    Christian's ch. Jacob Gocker: Johanna Berger: Jacob Kockert: Hans-George
    Cleiss: Wendel Schenk.
    Hasse 51 52 56 81 116 123 171 174 190 204 220 306 322 357 358 378 386 396 395
         422 426 452 468 486 510 575 578 606 651 702 752 756 761 785
264 HASSE: John, Bethlehem 20/5/1797-26/6/1797 Anna Maria w X. mens 4 ch. sil
    Joseph Oerter of Bethlehem, John Lehnert, Rossie Ros W
265 HASSEL: *Elias, L. Saucon twp 6/5/1756-14/6/1756 mens "s" and Jacob. Anthony
    Lerch and Melchior (read John Melchor) X. Johan Berger, Wend Shenk W
    Hassen 29
    Haucher 12
    Hauck 103 174 485
    Hauke 32
    Haupt 14
    Hause 449
    Hausel 530
    Hauser 801
266 HAUSKNECHT: *Jacob, Towamensing twp 30/12/1780-(?) Anna Catharina w. mens
    Martin, Catharine (9 yrs), Mary-Barbara et al. Nicholas Kern. M. Younge W
    Hauss 299
267 HAUSSEN: Casper. Henry Hauser and David Strauss X. John Erdman and Bartel
    Shablie W
    Hausser 267
    Havelly 317
    Hawk 776
268 HAYCOCK: Jeremiah, Chestnuthill twp yeoman 27/12/1796-19/1/1797 Sarah w X. ch
    (Jpacher), Josiah, Richard, Rosanna, Thomas, Mary, Hannah, William, Nathan,
    Martha, Amos, Jane. mens ld of Michael Poots (Butz). John Penrose of Rich-
    land, Bucks X. Everard Foulk, William and Jesse Haycock W
    Haycock 541
    Hayl 189
269 HAYS: John, Allen twp. 9/4/1783-16/3/1790 Jean w X. ch William, John, Esbel,
    Mary, Elizabeth, (Wilson, James, Robert, Jane (Brown), Francis, Esbel(Patten
    Mary, (Gray). mens Jane Rosburg: John Dunlys: Thos. Boyd: John Hays jr.
    Robert Hays. John s X and Nigel Gray X. Conrad Kreider and John Allison W
    (Robert's eldest s John)
    Hays 74 93 210 340 347 397 433 627 743
    Hazlet 442
    Heber 32 195

270 HEBERLY: Adam junior, Whitehall, yeoman 3/3/1791-9/5/1791 Anna Barbara w.
ch Adam (under 15 yrs), Margaret, Maria-Barbara, Maria-Elizabeth. mens
"his parents living". lds of Jacob Hamman, Peter Good, George Rup, George
Schneider, Henry Stetler, Leonard Meyer, Jacob Heberly, Philip Knouse.
George-Frederick Knause and John Roth jr X. Jacob Hamman and Peter Guth W
Heberly 270 706
Heckenboden 456
Heckenwelder 486 519 701 734
Hecker 126 284
Heckman 50 411 436

271 HECTER: Casper, L. Saucon twp 10/5/1780-20/12/82 mens John Casper Smith s of
John Smith of Springfield, Bucks. "the ch of his 3 dau-in-law" Adam Cucker
of L. Saucon X and guar. Geo Edelman W

272 HEENIG: *Jacob, Moore twp 8/9/1777-(?) Anna-Margrata w. Adam Dreisbach of
Lehigh X. Philip *Heyny and George Brown W

273 HEFFELFINGER: Henry. (?)-12/3/1796 8 ch. Jacob Strein, George Flickinger,
Anthony Deshler W
Heffelfinger 39 192 294 800
Hehl 231 460
Heiberger 779
Heidsman 259
Heilman 726
Heimbach 132 191
Heinkle 595

274 HEINTZELMAN: George (?)-30/9/1794 Adam Miller X and W. Handeter Heintzelman W
Helffuch 296 762
Helfrich 714
Helick 175

275 HELLER: Simon, Hamilton twp 18/5/1785-21/6/1785 Margareth w. ch Daniel"(ld in
Hamilton where Simon now lives to pay 300 pounds for it"), John, Jacob
(given "place in Plainfield"), Simon, Caty, Abraham, Michael, Veronica, Mary,
Elizabeth, Margareth, Sarah, Lovis, Anthony. "overseer of will" Michael
Bossert, Christopher Heller, Jacob Steelsmith W. (see Eyerman's Genealogical
Studies)

276 HELLER (Keller): *Joseph Plainfield, yeoman. 7/3/1797-21/10/1800 Mary Engle w X.
mens s Simon X, Joseph X, Jacob X, Philip (youngest s), lds of Leonard Kern
and Christian Bender. John Young, Christian Bender, Jacob Heller W
Heller 133 179 245 250 325 365 394 416 456 516 612 750
Hellman 308
Helman 301

277 HEMBDT: Jacob, Easton, tavernkeeper 10/5/1792-27/1/1796 Barbara w X. mens
Barbara d of his bro Casamund; friend and neighbor Robert Traill X Jacob
Sickman, John Arndt jr, Frederick Gwinner, and Peter Righter W
Hembt 703
Hemphill 73
Hendrix 176
Heneke 747
Henky 221
Henry 91 162 177 254 457 470 530 539 601 718 733 764 765

278 HENSLER: Margareth, wid of Christian 1/2/1781-23/11/1781 Friend Peter Rhoads X
and legatee. George Groff "drew will" No W
Hentz 446

279 HEPPLER: Casper, Up Milford 29/4/1769-1/8/1769 Anna Mary w. Bernhard Winsh X, Michael Sheible X. Sebastian Truckenmiller W
280 HERBELL: Christophel, Up Saucon, joiner 17/3/1760-31/3/1760 mens bro Peter Herbell (iss). John Appell X. Philip Buckeker, W. Christian Bachman and George (?) W
Herbell 280
Herbert 217
281 HERMAN: Conrad, Lehigh twp ("old age") 8/1/1797-14/11/1798 Augustina Maria w. ch mens Lawrence, George X, Jacob X, Conrad. mens lds of Peter Anthony, John Shneider, George Livegood and the heirs of Lewis Kister, Jacob Kuntz, John Schweb W
Herman 130 205 316 390 418 672 745
Hermany 238 514 573 641 772
Hern 598
Herner 239
Heron 430
Herr 8
282 HERRON: Thomas, Moore twp. 11/6/1772-19/11/1772 Jean w X. mens William McConnel (s of his wf Jean). Rev John Rosbrugh; Mary Fleming of Moore; "his bro of Moor's Arthur Lattimore of Allen yeoman co-X. Thomas Likens, Joseph Likens and Henry Newton W
Herron 74 102 535
Herter 37
Hertel 107
Herster 739
283 HERTZELL: Jacob, Bethlehem 3/1/1781-6/4/1781 Barbara w X. ch Jonas (eldest), X, Philip, Jacob, John, Regena, Christina, Elizabeth, Molly, ThomasHartman, Baltzer Stahl Sr and Jr W
284 HERTZEL: George, L Saucon 21/2/1757-3/2/1762 Catharine w. ch. Johann-Edidius Hecker and Jacob Shymer W
Hertzel 15 326 513 555 586 605 729 754
285 HERTZOG: *Peter, Salisbury 14/5/1777-(?) "annamira" w X. Mathias Albert, Christ, Giss W
Hesler 726
286 HESS: John Conrad, N. Britain, Bucks 5/7/1773-6/1/1797 Jacob Batzel, George Scholl W
287 HESS: Frederick, Lynn twp 25/1/1769-23/3/1769 Anna Margaretta w X. s David. mens Catharine, Philip, Elizabeth, Christina. Conrad Billman co-X. Thomas Everett and Michael Beck W
Hess 125 323 544
Hettler 473
288 HEYL: John, senior, Lynn twp 4/6/1798-13/11/98 John Heyl X. Samuel Everett, Philip Toselman W
Heyman 591
Heymer 728
Hilderbrand 134
289 HILGERT: Francis, Up Mt Bethel, yeoman 16/5/96-21/9/1797 Christina w. ch Peter X, Isaac, John, George, Ann-Mary (w of Abraham Houck), Jacob, Catharina (w of Adam Man(u)ny), and the wid and 4 ch of my s Abraham, decd. Friend Jacob Rick co-X. Dietrick Berg, Cathn *Berg, Hugh Foresman W
Hill 28
290 HILLEGAS: Michael, Up Saucon 10.10/1782-2/11/82 Cathrina w X. ch Anna-Margareth, Rebecca, John, Elisabeth, Michael, Eve, Catharina, Ann-Mary, John(minor). bro John Hillegas co-X. Abraham Backman and Daniel Cooper W

291 HILLAMN: Aaron, L Smithfield 14/4/1777-19/5/1777 Judah w X. ch John (eldes s),
    Elizabeth, Rachael,. Aaron,. Joseph; bro John Hillman coK. Beniah Mundy,
    Jacob Cuntraman, John Wayne W
    Hillman 299 307 611
    Hillyard 456 649
    Hirte 797

292 HITTEK: *Michael, senior, Salisbury, cordwainer 15/11/1783-26/1/1786 Ann Mary
    w. ch Michael (eldest s), John-Adam X, Frederick, Catharine (w of Geo
    Knappenberger), Margaret (w of Jacob Markel), George, Elizabeth (w of William
    Evans), Bartholomew, Magdalene (w of Leonard Rishel), Christina (w of Michael
    Ehrhard), Jacob, Barbara ("eldest dau mar John Hartzel, who now being
    deceased and left 5 ch Elizabeth, Geo-Adam Hartzell Mary Susannah and Leah,
    and my said dau is since married again") sil George Knappenberger co-X.
    George Kriebel, of Up Milford, yeoman, George Lautenschlaeger, Elias Weber W
    Hittel 232

293 HOCH (Hoog): Jacob 12/3/1789-18/3/1789 Franz Gainly X. Peter Obershymer X.
    Andreas and Johannis Reehrig W
    Hoocker 21

294 HOEFFELFINDER: *Magdalena 19/5/1799-10/6/1799 George Helfrich and Michael
    Best X. Anton Peter and Christian Bestsch W

295 HOENIG: Bernhard, Macungie, blacksmith 4/6/1795-11/8/1795 Susanna w. ch Henry
    (eldest: minor), Bernhard (minor), George, Susanna, Catherine, Geo-Frederick
    Knauss X, Jacob Mohr X(app. declined as letters adm. issued to wid and George
    Gor of Macungie) Herman Hartman, John Soder W
    Hoff 216 231

296 HOFFMAN: George 22/11/1789-3/3/1790 John Helfrich and Nicholas Sietzelberger W

297 HOFFMAN: Michael, Whitehall, yeoman 20/1/1777-12/1/1787 ch John X, Michael,
    Maria-Magdalena (w of Peter Bear of Heidelberg), Juliana (w of Henry Smith of
    Heidelberg), Maria-Barbara (w of Samuel W-otering of Whitehall). Adan von
    Erd, J. Okely and William Boehler W

298 HOFFMAN: Christian (intestate) 16/3/1796-1/19/1800 Jno Hartman X. George
    and Geo-Jacob Horn W
    Hoffman 19 164 200 566 697 699
    Hofmer 259

299 HOLBE: Silvester, Lynn twp 6/7/1779-(?) Clara w. youngest s Christian and
    Jacob. mens step-s William Holbe: sil Peter Weiss; sil Jacob Grim; sil John
    Briner. Geo-Michael Kuntz X. Christian Sieberling X. John Hilman and Carl
    and Jacob Hauss W
    Holbe 615 769 770
    Holber 617
    Holder 197 382 498
    Holland 554 793
    Hollinshead 411
    Holmes 428
    Holtz 648

300 HOLTZHAUSEN: *Henry, Delaware twp 27/3/1787-20/4/1787 (read Up Milford, yeoman
    26/4/1787-15/5/1787 Barbara "present w" ch Jacob (eldest s), Catharine (eldest
    dau, w of Conrad Gillan and iss Susanna et al), John, Susanna, Barbara, Mary.
    bil by 1st w Jacob Stahl X, Jacob Brobst X. Casper Rieser, Jno *Dieter
    Miller W
    Holtzhauser 649
    Hood 3

Hoover* 96 97 140 792
Hopron 163 231
Hering 222
Horlacher 47 48
Horn 54 184 225 298 313 325 404 407 411 673 724

301 HORNER: James, senior, Allen twp yeoman 20/4/1791-6/5/1793 ch Hugh X, Thomas,
Jenny, John, Sarah (w of William McNair), Mary, James, mens lds of Conrad
Laubach, Simon Dreisbach, David Blackey, Christian Holman, Anthony
Clippinger, Jacob Bear, Thomas Wilson and William McNair. nephew Joseph
Horner co-X James Kerr, John Allison and James Allison W
Horner 13 149 216 361 366 399 402 440 546 560 561 617 637 664 671 726 782
Horning 730

302 HORSFIELD: Timothy, Bethlehem, physician 22/7/1788-6/6/1789 Julianna w X guar.
bros Joseph Horsfield and Joseph Otto X, and guar. mens William and Thomas;
John Ettwein; Paul Munster; bro Israel: bro Joseph; sis Anna (w of Joseph
Otto): sis Elizabeth (w of Henry Lyndenmeyer): sil Johann Garrison.
Codicil 28/7/1788 mens Anna Maria Demuth of Bethlehem. Tobias Boeckel Frantz
Thomas, Peter Vetter 2 W to both
Horsfield 417 487 510 29 79 156 231 358
Horter 19

303 HORSFIELD: Timothy, Bethlehem 4/8/1722=7/5/73 mens Mary w X. sis Anna Leadbetter
of New York X. Timothy X, Joseph X, Ann-Mary X, Israel X, Elizabeth X.
Abraham Andreas, A. Boemper and J. Okely W

304 HOUCK: Dietrich, Williams twp yeoman 10/12/1784-2/5/1789 ch Maria-Catarina
(eld dau), Maria-Anna, Margereta (youngest dau), Abraham X, Simon. Benetick
Lutz co-X, John Beyl, Daniel Reinheimer, George-Heinrich Unangst W
Houck 289
Houk 467
Houser 6 459
Housram 180
Howell 46

305 HOWER: Friderick, Allen twp yeoman 8/1/1791-17/8/1797 Mary Elizabeth w X. ch
John-Nicholas, X, John, Mary; mens Charles Haffey. Henneckel Hower, William
Kromer decd) and Peter Buche W
Hower 111
Hrobbenberger 106

306 HUBER: George (?)-31/3/1790 Ann Mary X, George X, mens Frederick Marshall.
Jacob Rubel, John Hasse W
Huber 154 166 201 235 468 478 736

307 HUBLER: *Barbara, L Mt Bethel wid of Jacob of Plainfield 17/6/1795-16/1/1796
ch Jacob, Frederick, Christina, (w of Michael Closs), Gottlich, Rosanna (w of
Ch Hillman), John, Abraham X. John Mill, Joseph Martin and John Mill senior W

308 HUBLER: Jacob, Plainfield 4/5/1789-9/5/1789 Barbara w. ch Jacob (eldest),
Frederick, Gottlieb, John, Abraham), Isaac X, Mens "father's estate in
Germany, Hans-Jacob Hoebler": gddau Magdalena Hellman. Jacob Eyerly jr John
Schaeffer and George Schwartz W
Hubler 682

309 HUEBNER: Johann Ludwig (?)-27/9/1796 mens "bond of John Bonn" John Shropp,
Joseph Oerter W
Huebner 51 222 421 512

310 HUFSMITH: Peter, Hamilton twp 8/3/1794-24/3/94 Mary w. ch Adam), Henry X,
Catharan, Elizabeth Margaret. mens Henry Putz(Buth). Philip Grasya,
Cornelius Bellesfiet W

Hugh 424

EQQ HUGHES: Thomas, Lebanon, soldier 27/4/1758-17/6/1765 Mary w. mens "to receive prize-money from the paymaster of N.J. Regiment". bros Richard Hughes and John Stooksberry: sis Unis Stooksberry. John Hanna, Henry Hansen W

Hugus 36 466

312 HUMEL: Elias (?)-1/8/1794 Adam and Elias Humel X Martin Rauch, George Beck W

313 HUNSICKER: *John. Casper and Jacob Hunsicker X (prob 17/12/1800) George Bloss, Jacob Peter and George Horn W

Hunsicker 509 538 633 794

Hunsperger 327

Hunt 176

Hunter 499

Hurlocker 76

Husse 632

Huston 209 678

314 HUTCHINSON: James, Lehigh twp yeoman 2/10/1780-24/5/1784 Mary w X. ch James, William, Mary, Esther, Sarah, Margareth. Robert Lattimore X Wm Stewrd, Margareth *Stewrd, Mary Stop W

Hutchinson 58 329 535

315 HUTH: Conrad, Williams twp cordwainer 11/5/1799-31/5/1799 ch William, Margaret, Elizabeth, Magdalena, Susanna. Jacob Overly X and sil Henry Unangst X, both of L Saucon. Henry Ohl and Nicholas Klein W

Hyndshaw 616

Ihrie 11 28 100 101 175 188 411 412 477 534 615 654 764

Ingoldt 566

Innes 464 720

Jacoby 3 424 663

Jacobs 170

Jane 318

Janson 121

Jaques 348

316 JARRETT: Isaac, Macungie, husbandman 8/6/1790-17/7/1790 Catharine w. ch John (eldest s), X, Daniel X, Jacob, Henry, Isaac, Gertrude and "three youngest dau". mens lds of Jacob Herman, Lawrence Hern, Matthias Weshego, Jacob Meier, Mathias Equer, Jacob Stephon, Jacobvan Buskirk and Ferdinand Wertz. Jacob Mohr, Mathias Wesgo W

317 JARRETT: John, Macungie, Bucks 22/3/1752-15/12/1755 ch John X, Samuel, Philip, Daniel, William, Isaac, Sebastian, Edward, Mary (Hevelly), Elizabeth (Turny), Jone, Margareth, Sarah. George Derr and Johannes Reiss W

318 JAYNE: *Timothy, L Smithfield, farner 14/12/1780(9)-30/3/1790 Sarah w X, John, Timothy, Daniel, William, Rebecka, Anne (w of David Ogden), Sarah, Catherine, Ebenezer, Isaac and Elizabeth Jayne W

Jayne 257 291 318

319 JENNINGS: *Solomon, Salisbury, yeoman 4/6/1755-3/3/1757 ch John (eldest s), X, Rachael, Elisabeth, Isaiah X, Susanne, Ezekiel, Judith, sil Nicholas Scull co-X. Lewis Klotz et al W

Jennings 144 432

Jentzer 182

320 JERION: *Mathias, Lynn tsp yeoman 6/11/1761-24/5/1763 Magdalena w X. ch George (eldest s), Conrad X, Elizabeth, Jacob; Mathias Romig, David Bulman and Adam Romig W

321 JOHNSON: David, Millerstwon 6/1/1785-3/3/1785 mens Mary w. Jacob s. bil
     Alexander McMichael X Michael Schaeffer, Philip Muhling W
322 JOHNSON: Just, Bethlehem, tobacconist 4/6/1790-17/7/1790 Mary Magdalen w X.
     "only ch" Maria-Justina. mens lease of Fredk Marshall. John Hasse co-X.
     guar Tobias Boeckel. Frantz Thomas W
323 JOHNSON: *Christopher, Up Saucon 29/7/1801-12/9/1801 Mary Catharina w X. ch
     Daniel, Henry, Christopher, David, Jacob, Caty, John, Polly, Betsy, Lydea,
     Susanna. sil Philip Hess (hus of "Caty")/ bil Adam Shoener, John Green,
     Peter Myer W. mens lds in Moore and Springfield twp
     Johnson 99 245 582
324 JOHNSON: *Mary, Mt Bethel "widower" 17/8/1785-27/1/1786 mens Rebekah dau.
     Samuel s X. Josiah Raymond, James Beard, Thomas Ross W
325 JONES: John, Bethlehem, blacksmith 5/3/1781-21/6/1781 Eleanor w X. mens John
     ("indenture made 5/9/1776"): Johannes (as a female): slave Susannah: "Levy
     Jones, ellegitimate s of my s Levy; my said son's Levy's widow, having child
     by him, and having (?) from this state" Note of 2d s Gritfith, dated 23/6/1778:
     gds Grith fith, s of Jesse: gddau Hannah and Rebecca ch of Jesse: gds Joseph
     Jones of N. Carolina, eldest s of decd s Jonathan: Note given by Jonathan to
     his father 18/12/1769: (jonathan had 2 day): 4th s Peter: 5th s Thomas:
     Sarah Hornber: gds John s of Joseph: 7th s Joseph X: lds of Patrick Grame
     (conveyed to 325, 4/4/1750 in Willialiams twp., adj lds of Daniel Reinhard:
     lds of Peter and Elizabeth Miller adj Joseph Grove and Lodowick Heller
     (conveyed 13/2/1776). John Hasse and Tobias Boeckel W (6th s John) and gds
     Jesse s of Thomas
     Jones 70 108 223 497 508 636 733
     Juncker 94
326 KACHLEIN: Peter, Esquire, Easton. 7/11/1789-21/12/1789 Catharine w. mens Peter
     s (given lds in Forks, purchased of Robert Correy); Susanna dau (w of Peter
     Shnyder); Jacob s: Elizabeth dau; Andrew (youngest s. had Peter and Andrew);
     sil Peter Shnyder X, John Young X, Christopher Hertzel X, Robert Traill W,
     Jacob Arndt jr W Peter Shnyder W Frederick Barthold W Frederick Gwinner W.
     (For complete genealogy of this most prominent figure in Colonial and
     Revolutionary Northampton, see Eyerman's Genealogical Studies.
     Kachlein 38 550 594 654
     Kahler 792
     Kahn 602
     Kalberlahn 556
     Kalver 523
     Kampman 417
327 KAPPES: Jacob (?)-9/12/1794 Anna Kappes X, Isaac Kolb X, Ulrich Hunsperger,
     Jno-Adam Eyer W
     Karb 474
328 KARR: David, Plainfield 5/7/1763-19/2/1772 Mary w X. mens ch William X, Margaret
     (w of Timothy McCarty), Mary (w of George Santee), Jane (w of Thomas Orr),
     Elizabeth. Andrew Brocksch, Jacob Weissinger, John Okely W
329 KARR: David, Plainfield, weaver 5/7/1763-19/2/1772 Mary w X. ch Margaret lds
     of James Hutchinson.
     Kass 6
330 KAUFFMAN: George, Northampton 19/3/1798--/8/98 Elizabeth w. 6 ch incl George
     X. mens "inheritance from his father" mens Frederick Kauffman of "Upper
     Sal, near Berg on the Werra in Co of Totenbury, Hesse Rheinfels in Germany".
     Abraham Rincker of Northampton, hatter co-X, Jacob Newhard, George Graff, Peter
     Rhoads W

331 KAUP: *Valentine, Salisbury, yeoman 10/1/1786-21/2/1786 Susanna w X. mens
William (eldest S), George and Frederick ss. Hans-George Stufer co-X.
Philip Bergstressor, Nicholas Ueberroth W

332 KEAHLER: Sibila, Up Milford wid of Michael 13/10/1769-28/2/1770 ch mens
Cathrina, Elizabeth (w of Fredk Weisel), Sibilla, Jacob X. Peter Wetzell,
and Michael Eberhard W
Kearn 121
Kech 47 49 524 637 670
Kechly 664

333 KECK: Henry, senior, Salisbury, yeoman 8/5/1786-15/8/1786 ch John, George,
Henry, Frederick, Elizabeth (w of John Ritter), John Keck X. sil John
Ritter X. Peter Rhoads, Peter Newhart W

334 KECK: John, Heidelberg 1/5/1772-26/5/1772 Anna w X. mens Henry (youngest s),
John et al bro Henry coK. Johannes Miller, Henry Geigerist W

335 KECKEL:(UE), Michael, Macungie, yeoman 22/2/1763-29/3/1784 Magdalena, Elizabeth,
Margarata, Gartrout, Lovease. Godch Lovease dau of Michael Snyder,
Melchior Smith, William Haintz W
Keentz 6

336 KEGEL: Henry, Hamilton twp (?)-12/3/1789 mens George: Conrad Arnold, Mathias
Keonig, Bartel Scheibele W

337 KEINAT: Claudius, Macungie 8/3/1760-12/6/1760 mens w and iss. Ludwig Wagner,
Jacob Wetzel, George-Adam Bortz and Andrew Dressler W
Keiper 54

338 KELLER: Christopher, Hamilton, yeoman 27/5/95-5/8/1795 Christina w. ch George
X, Mary, Christopher, Catharine (w of Michael Butz), Susanna, Andrew. mens
lds of Peter Conrad and Simon Fries. Michael Bossert guar. Matthias Otto and
John Stout W
Keller (see 276)
Keller 133 276

339 KEMBLE: Elizabeth, Nazareth, wid of George. 7/5/1788-19/1/1789. mens husband's
2 dau, Anne and Eleanor: 4 gdch Francis, Rebecca, Thomas, Jacob; bros Jacob
Christ, August Schloesser; William-David Kennedy of Phila. Elizabeth Miss
dau X. Joseph Otto, J. Eyerly jr Geo Godfrey W
Kemer 457
Kemerer 84
Kempfer 541
Kempp 615 770
Kendel 509

340 KENEDY: *James, Lehigh twp yeoman, mason 1/3/1763-6/2/1764 Elizabeth w. ch
William, James, Mary, Margaret, Elizabeth, Thomas, Jacob, Sarah; mens William
Kennedy guar of dau Janet. John Hays and Thos Boyd X. Neigel Gray. Jas Hays W
Kennedy 339

341 KERN: William, Heidelberg twp (?)-26/6/1801 mens ch Salome and Christopher Kern ?
Jacob Strein, Henry Zerfass jr W
Kern 193 209 266 276 316 342 372 396 508 562
Kerr 9 10 141 301 567

343 KERSHNER: George, Richland twp widower 3/1/1793-18/4/1794 mens dau Julianna
(w of George Kernk had oldest s George-Jacob): dau Christina (w of Jacob
Kessler X. Daniel Weitner, Jacob Smith W

343 KESSLER: Leonhard 3/8/1785-20/9/1785 mens Salomon Fridrich: Christoph
Bittenbender Petrus Nungesses X. Robert Traill and Adam Dreisbach of Easton W

344 KESSLER: *Casper, L Saucon 1/11/1770-4/12/1778 Margaret w X. mens sil Baltzer
Weaver and Chris-ina. George Sterner W

Kessler 342 394 448
Keston 627
Ketter 627
Ketterer 492
Ketterman 407
Keyser 367

345 KIEFER: Mary, Salisbury twp (?)-23/8/1792. Charles Colver X, Isaac Clewell X.
Daniel Osterlein, John Wygand W

346 KIENLE: *Lawrence, Macungie, yeoman 19/3/1785-21/2/1785 mens ch Catherine,
Gertrude, Margaret, Valentine, George. Peter Trexler s of 'Squire Trexler'
X. William Smith X. Andreas Berger, John Doll W
Kiessers 71

347 KING: Mary, Allen twp 13/12/1789-12/3/1790 mens ch Jean (w of John Hays), Ann
(Lattimore), Christina (Ralston). gds William and James Lattimore: sil
John Ralston X: Sarah Ralston dau of Samuel, decd. "his bro Richard Walker":
gdch Gabriel and Lettice Ralston (d of Samuel). James Ralston and John McNair W
King 743
Kip 734

348 KIRK: Frederick, Allen twp 4/4/1797-15/5/1797 Elizabeth w X. and iss. Samuel
Funk, Jacob Baer, and John D. Jaques W

349 KIRSHBAUM: Philip, Penn twp 24/4/1772-10/6/1772 mens friend Dewalt Billman:
Maria-Clara Schoen, d of John-George Schoen. Thomas Everitt X. Philip
Wortman, Michael Habber W
Kirshner 342

350 KISTLER: Michael, Lynn twp (?)-13/8/1792 Daniel Kistler X. Philip Fosselman,
Philip Kistler W

351 KLEIN: *Andrew, Plainfield, yeoman 15/1/1786-1/2/1786 Jane Elizabeth w. mens 7
dau incl 2 youngest Sarah and Rachael. Johannes Klewald X Christopher Demuth
(bo n sil). William Edmonds Henry Gersten W
Kistler 281
Kleckman 369
Kleckner 572

352 KLEIN: Conrad. L Saucon, mason 12/12/1794-14/12/1797 Ursula w. ch Nicholas,
Michael X et al mens John Shuler. Peter Lerch Baltzer *Eckert W
Klein 50 164 351 315 356 360
Kleinhans 405 547

353 KLEINTOB: *John, Chestnuthill twp 22/3/1783-15/8/1785 Eve w X. John Kleintob co-
X Adam Englert, Valentine Meckes W
Kleipinger 134
Kleist 222 575 730 736 768

354 KLEPPINGER: John Henry, Allen twp yeoman 12/1/1790-9/2/1796 Anna Mary w. mens
ld in Moore: nephew John-George s of bro John of Southampton, Franklin Co
Pa. also had Henry and Mary): note of John Nagel: nephew Anthony s of bro
Lewis: nephew Henry s of bro Anthony; nephew Anthony s of bro Frederick:
Elizabeth Donart: ld of Mr Siegfried: bro George (iss): bil George and John
Nagel (both with iss): bil John Dreisbach: John Lerch Sr: bil Conrad Solt:
bil Jacob Solt: Frederick Nagel bil (all with iss). Ann Mary w X. John
Nagel X, John George X George Haas, Henry Deil W
Kleppinger 504
Klewald 351

355 KLEWELL: Frantz, Plainfield 2/10/1792-12/4/98 Salome w. ch John X, Julianna,
Frantz X, Nathaniel, Magdalena, Elizabeth, ch of Margaret decd., Ann-Mary,
Rosina, Christin-Salome, Dorel, Jacob Eyerly, jr, Joseph Levering (since
decd) W

356 KLICK: *Frederick, Salisbury, yeoman 30/1/1794-13/5/1794 Elizabeth w. ch
    Henry, Jacob, Samuel, Mary, Elizabeth, Philip, Catherine (minors). mens lds
    of Geo-Adam Blank; bro George K. of Whitehall X, bro Philip K of Albany twp X.
    Henry *Reichert, James Gill, Philip Klein W
    Kliess 395
357 KLEIST: Daniel, Bethlehem twp locksmith "the soldier" 6/11/1789-12/5/1792 mens
    Daniel ch of Bethlehem, locksmith X ch Anna-Rosina Kluss of Bethlehem, spinster
    X Frederick Marshall. Andrew Boerhek of Bethm X (since decd), John Hasse X.
    Jacob Rubel, Peter Ross, Jno Hasse W
    Klinat 337
358 KLINE: George, Bethlehem, yeoman 11/4/1783-29/7/1783 Dorothy w X (former wid of
    D. Eisenhart) mens kindswoman, Anna Bender of Bethm spinster; Andrew Eisenhart
    of Macungie: 3 bros Henry X, Michael X, Leonard X. kinswoman, An-Catherine
    Verbis: Catharina Merk w of Conrad Merk and dau of my bro Jacob decd. sis
    Elizabeth Eidler of Lancaster Co. ch of decd sis Anna Frantz: Daniel Neubert,
    friend and his wf. bro Leonard co-X. John-Christian Hasse co-X John Gruem,
    Timothy Horafield, Gottlieb Lange W
    Kline 767
359 KLINGSOHR: The Rev Johann August: (?)-22/1/1799 Anna Elisabeth w X. John
    Schropp X. John-Christian Reich, Rev Jacob van Vleck W
360 KLIPPEL: John, Williams twp yeoman 10/7/1764-1/3/1765 Anna Margrata w X. friend
    Jacob Reich X mens "ch of his only dau Mary-Margrata w of Philip Opp". John
    Koer, Rossannah Clyne, Elizabeth *Moor W
361 KLOTZ: John, senior, Lowhill twp yeoman 10/7/1764-(read 19/12/1795-13/1/1796)
    ch John, John-George, Jacob", Christian", Daniel", Maria-Barbara**, Maria-
    Magdalena**, Maria-Catharina**, Susanna**, mens lds of Michael Deiber, Tobias
    Messer, Jacob Resh, Jacob Lesser, Geo Krauss, Sebastian Edel, Peter Knedler,
    Jacob Horner and Andrew Knerr. Geo Stern, Geo Knodler W (" under 15 yrs.
    ** under 18 yrs)
    Klotz 18 64 131 319 388 414 474 515 602 675 714 777 778 779
    Klust 357
    Knaepple 502
    Knappeley 49
    Knappenberger 292
    Knapply 559
362 KNAUSS: Gottfried, Whitehall, yeoman 25/3/1763-(?) Regina Louisa w X. ch Gottfried,
    Francis, Daniel, Conrad, Paul, Henry, John, David, Lizabeth. "his w had by her
    1st hus, 2 ch Peter and Susanna": bro George Knauss co-X and guar. Andreas
    Broshsch, John Okely W
363 KNAUSS: Godfreyd, Whitehall 25/3/1763-21/3/1777 (same as above in all respects
    but mens 10th ch Margaret and W Andreas Brorhack, Jacob Messinger and J. Okely)
364 KNAUSS: John, Up Milford weaver 26/1/1761-12/6/1761 Maria-Catharina w X. bro
    Sebastian Knauss X son Michael. J. Okely, Bernard Wench, Andreas Gering,
    George-Adam Haun W
    Knauss 164 229 270 295 375 377 500 508 577 627 628 677 701 707 778
365 KNECHT: Peter, L Saucon 3/3/1773-27/3/1773 ch George-Henry, eldest X, Ulrich,
    Leonard X, Anna-Barbara (w of Detrick Heller), Anna-Christina w. mens lds of
    Rudolph Oberly. Michael Lutts, Rudolph Oberly, Jacob Christman W

    Knecht 492 640
    Kneibel 560
    Knepley 179

366 KNERR:* *Abraham, Lowhill twp yeoman 2/2/1790-3/5/1793 "dau yet living, Barbara
      Horner, Maria-Eve Fenstermacher, Anna-Barbara Giess, Susanna Hartman, Dorothy
      Stettler and 2 sons John and Andrew Knerr. mens gdch of eldest s Christopher,
      decd. Andrew, Barbara, Susanna, Maria-Eve: gdch of decd s Abraham, Abraham,
      Anna, Elizabeth, Susanna. Jacob Horner X, Philip Stettler X, P. Kocher W
      Knerr 361 462
      Knight 363
367 KNOBLOCH: Henry 1787-19/6/1788 Peter Keyse X Daniel Schmeier, John Romich W
      Knoedler 361
368 KNOUSE: Sebastian, Salisbury (Emmaus) 24/2/1777-(?) Anna Catharina w X. ch
      John, Jacob, Abraham, Lewis, Philip, Catharina (w of Conrad Ernst), Anna-Mary
      (Mayer), Elizabeth (w of Fredk Romich), Magdalena, Ann-Johanna, Henry X,
      Andreas Giring X
      Koaler 375
369 KOCK: *Maria Sarah, Allen twp wid of John 30/4/1791-31/1/1794 mens Elizabeth
      (w of Jacob Meyer), Barbara (w of Jacob Kleckner), Catherine (w of Bastian
      Wolf), Christina, decd, John-George X, Daniel, gddau Sarah Neblig "only sur
      ch of dau Christina decd" mens note of Abraham and Sanuel Landes. sil Jacob
      Meyer of Pittsburgh, guar os Sarah. Jacob Meyer co-X Samuel Landes, James
      Brown W
370 KOCH: *John, Allen twp yeoman 27/5/1777-13/12/1782 Maria Sarah w X, ch John-
      George, Daniel, Elizabeth (w of Jacob Meyer), Barbara, Catherine, Christina;
      Robert Craig, A. Boemper, Abraham Andreas, J. Okely W
      Koch 180 199 200 461 523 524 569 578 656 703 744
      Kocher 144 297 366 457 569 599 611
371 KOCKERT: Adam, L Saucon farmer 11/9/1797-28/12/1799 Elizabeth w. mens Daniel
      Weiknecht s of sis Mary-Catherine: Jacob Kockert s of bro Jacob; Daniel
      Weitknecht: Simon Dreisbach: Adam Stephen: Adam and Elizabeth ch of Peter
      Laubach; Adam and Elizabeth ch of Conrad Laubach: Adam, Elizabeth and Fred-
      erick ch of Frederick Laubach: sis Mary-Catharine (w of Michael Laubach)
      Michael Laubach of Mt Bethel X, Daniel Weitknecht and Jacob Lach of L Saucon X
      Henry Ohl, George Stuber, Felix Lynn W
      Kockert 263 605
      Koder 94
372 KOEHLER: George, Whitehall, blacksmith 3/7/1797-3/6/1799 Mary Elisabeth w. mens
      sis Margaret-Catharina (w of Jacob Dengler): sis Christina (w of Jacob Miller):
      "and unto the daughters of sister Hannah Mack: George Frantz s of Jacob
      Frantz: George Fenstermacher s of half-bro William: nephew George and Peter
      Smell: 6 sis of my wf Catharina, Sabinah, Margaret, Eve, Barbara and Mary"
      Peter Rhods trustee. George Rhoads of Northampton X, Nicholas Kern of White
      hall X. Abraham Rinker, Matthias Swink and John Moll W
      Koehler 27 90 373 497
      Koehnig 295 336 786
      Kogel 198
373 KOHLER: Peter, Whitehall, Esquire 5/8/1793-15/10/1793 Julianna w. Peter "only
      s". bro Jacob Kohler and bil George Graff X and guar. Peter Rhoads (jr:sr:),
      Jacob Schreiber W
      Kohler 192 253 255 256 418 621 697
      Kokal 559
      Kolbe 327 796
      Kooken 84 172 218 252 674 779
      Kooker 271 776

374 KOON: Margaret (?)-3/12/1773 ch John (eldest), Henry, Mary, Ann-Margaret. mens
    ch of Peter Ruffner. Peter Road, Margaret Kun, John Gressemer, Casper
    Schunenbruch
    Koon 779 788
    Koplin 465 708

375 KOPP: Samuel Eberhard, Up Milford, potter 7/2/1757-26/2/1757 mens s Philip-
    Christopher Keup: sil Michael Wolfgeuch; sil Michael Nipsi (?) John Knowes and
    Gabriel Koaler X. Thomas Owens, Johannes Koehler W. Renunciation of X,
    wit by William Parsons and Just Vollert
    Kortz 589 792
    Kraft 466

376 KRAM: Jacob, L Saucon, miller 22/4/1798-8/5/98 Barbara w ch Jacob X, Peter,
    Abraham X, John, Henry, Catharine, Susanna. John Geisinger X John Beyl, Samuel
    and Rothrock W
    Kram 507
    Kraemer 729
    Krames 447
    Krammer 748
    Krammes 129
    Krauss 361 568 789

377 KRATZER: Philip, Up Milford, yeoman 5/1782-13/5/1788 Elizabeth w. ch Frederick
    (eldest s), Benjamin, Jacob; stepks Henry Dauber. George Sobert X of Salisbury,
    blacksmith and Henry Knauss X of Salisbury, wheelright. Abraham Ziegler,
    Frederick Winsch W

378 KRAUSSE: Heinrich (?)-18/5/1792 mens lease of Frederick Marshall John Krausse X,
    Jacob Schuck X. John Hasse and John Krausse of Beth. W. Codicil W by Peter
    Youngman and Christian Eggest.
    Kreamer 178

379 KREGLOH: Henry /1786-23/7/1787 Barbara X John George, John Sieger W
    Kreibel 695
    Kreider 269 518 627 658
    Kreiter 170
    Kremser 249

380 KRESS: *Charles 18/10/1792-27/11/1792. Catharina-Margaretha w. John-Jacob
    Leinenberger X Michael Kuester (read Nicholas) and Anton Petri
    Kress 432
    Kretz 388
    Kriebel 292 561 789
    Krieber 754
    Kribel 396
    Krible 568
    Kroeage 147
    Krogstrop 231
    Krom 406
    Kromer 157 251 410 305 504 726

381 KROMLEY: Adam, Moore twp 8/3/1773-1/5/1773 Margaret w X. ch Franc (only s by
    pres w) X. mens 5 ch by 1st w (pres w had ch by former hus.) George Clavell,
    Christ. Spaengler W
    Krubel 523

382 KRUM: Anthony: Lynn twp 21/11/1764-18/10/1765 Cattrout w. John-Henry et al.
    Joseph Holder, Andrew Meyer, John Everitt W
    Krumdein 465
    Kuckert 405

Kuehel* 625

383 KUFFT: George, Up Milford, weaver 7/2/1779-4/7/1780 ch of his dau Margreta (w
of Baltzer Fatherman X), John Philip, John, Barbara, Susanna and Saloma
Fatherman. Frederick Limbach and John Schant W

384 KUHN: Frederick, Forks twp yeoman 5/10/1785-12/4/1790 Ana w. sons Abraham,
Isaac, Jacob, John, Stephen, Catharin (w of Fredk Wagner). mens lds of Fredk
Wilhelm, Jacob Peiffer. Peter Sayler X Jacob Arndt jr, Robert Traill, William
Kous (Roup)W

385 KUGLER: Johann Philip 25/1/1796-21/1/1797 George Laudenberger W
Kuhn 106 374 781

386 KUNCKLER: *Daniel, Bethlehem, tobacconist 3/8/1776-6/7/1779 Anna Maria w X.
ch Sarah, Daniel X Charles, Peter. mens Nathaniel Seidel, Francis Thomas
guar. Ephriam Colves, Tobias Boechel, John Hasse W
Kunckell 449
Kunkel 583

387 KUNKELL: Laurence (?)-20/19/1800 David Strauss X Jno Williams X. Conrad Wetzell,
John Strauss W
Kuntz 8 21 33 40 281 299 585 638 694 699 780
Kuntzman 173 798

388 KURR: Henry, Up Milford 2/2/1761-22/7/1761 Eve-Magdalena w X. 6 ch incl Peter.
gds John-Jost Kretz. Lewis Klotz co-X

389 KURTZ: George, Allen twp 7/10/1787-20/10/1787 "nuncupative" Elizabeth w. s George
and his sisters. John Steiner, Henry Patterson W
Kurtz 12
Kuesler 380
Kushkl 29

390 KUESTER: Ludwig, Lehigh twp yeoman 11/12/1786-20/10/1787 (read 29/1/1787)
Catherine w. Peter Anthony jr X and Conrad Herman X of Lehigh twp yeoman.
Conrad Herman, P. Anthony Sr W
Kystand 478

391 LABAR: Abraham, Easton, tailor 18/12/1777-29/4/1791 Rosina w X. mens bros Daniel
and George Labar. Robert Traill, Mchl Yohe, J-Nich Troxell

392 LABAR: Charles, Up Mt Bethel, yeoman 6/4/1790-24/5/1790 Margaret w. ch George,
Abraham, Daniel, Leonora, William, Margaret, Sarah, Mary, Jacob Beck X,
Christian Smith of Up Mt Bethel, X. Melchoir *Labar, John Fauner W

393 LABAR: William senior Up Mt Bethel yeoman Elizabeth w. ch John X, William,
Elias, Peter, Charles, Philip, Daniel, Catharine, Mary, Barbara, Margaret.
sil Jonas Smith co-X. John Faunce, George and Daniel Labar W
Labar 550 553 569 667 793
Lachenour 406

394 LADEMACHER: John, L Saucon, yeoman 16/5/1793-20/6/1793 Barbara w. mens dau
Elizabeth (w of Peter Kessler), dau Catharine (w of "dudwiler") dau Ann-
Elizabeth (w of David Heller). ch of dau Mary, decd. late w of Michael Rath.
also mens "his gdch" friend Anthony Lerch of L Saucon X. Paul Lerch, David
Lerch W
Laffer 126 453
Laird 723
Landon 96
Langdale 229
Lander 369
Landes 74 369

395 LANGE: Gottlieb, Bethlehem, saddler 1/10/1788-18/11/1791 mens "only s Christian" X. stepch John, James and Elizabeth Hall: his w of James Hall: Nathaniel Seidel and Frederick Marshall of Bethm. "only dear ch Christian". his father, George Lange of Hartmansdorf, near Leipsig, in Saxony, Germany. Rebecca-Louisa dau of John-Christian Hasse. John-Ch Hasse X Anreas Borhek, Gottlieb Brown, Danl Kleiss jr W
Lane 97
Lanius 608 802
Lanke 247
Lange 358
Lanterman 731
Lantz 554
Larash 565
396 LAROSS: *Lodowog, Up Milford, cordwainer 17/3/1784-1/6/1784 Cininigunda (?) w. ch Henry (nar), Nicholas (oldest s), Joseph, Margrat (w of Geo. Morgan), Jacob, Susanna (w of Mathias Westgo), Regina (w of Nicholas Gift). Lodowog Shaler X, Mathias Kern X, Tobias Maechlin, George Kribel W
Laros 2
Larosh 773
397 LARR: *Martin, Plainfield 11/3/1799-28/5/1799 mens Elizabeth: "Two fathers Maria Katharina Eaquel, my fath Elizabeth and her s John Hays: my fath Susuna". ch Abraham X, Jacob X, William Maria, Elizabeth, Jacob Brotzman, Isaac Hertzell
Lash 767
398 LATHROPP: Frances 6/3/1754-15/6/1763 mens gdch James and his sis Lathropp Cruickshank: dau Elizabeth Dinly: dau Mary Cruickshank
399 LATTIMORE: *Arthur, Allen twp 9/3/1785-25/6/85 mens his mother X: bros Robert, William and John: contracts with Joseph Horner and my aunt Ester Burke. Joseph Horner, Moses Cougelton W
400 LATTIMORE: William, Allen twp yeoman 23/2/1795-20/3/1795 Christian w X. 2 ch Elizabeth, John, friend and cous William Lattimore co-X John McNair, Joseph Burk W
401 LATTIMORE: John, Allen twp 21/1/1797-2/2/1797 Margaret w. dau Elizabeth. mens bil James and Samuel Culberton. uncle John McNair Sr X John Wilson X, Christian Hagenbuch, Adam Clendinen
402 LATTIMORE: *Elizabeth, Allen twp 22/10/1792-24/10/1792 ch Robert (had Elizabeth), William, John. sis Martha and Esther. Joseph Horner X Adam Clendinen, Thomas Yuing (?) W
403 LATTIMORE: *Mary 6/2/1788-6/3/1788 mens dau Elizabeth Lattimore: cous Ann Craig: Elizabeth, George and John ch of Robert Lattimore jr. and his w Margaret: cous William Lattimore jr. cous Elizabeth Craig jr. John McNair Sr X. George Palmer, Hugh Wilson W
Lattimore 10 87 88 102 282 314 347 545 546 567
404 LAUB: Jacob (?)-8/6/1789 John Moritz X, George Horn X. Jacob and George Fluckinger W
405 LAUBACH: Christian, L Saucon, blacksmith 4/3/1768-5/1/1769 Susannah-Catherina w. ch John-George X, Elizabeth (w of Adam Kuckert), Conrad, Frederick, Reinhart, Peter; Rudoph and John Oberly, GeorheKhenry Kleinhans, J. Okely W purchased lands of George Riegel
Laubach 166 192 301 371 416 516
Laudenberger 384

406 LAUGENOR: *Christian, Heidelberg 12/3/1796-14/1/1799 John Krome, Peter
    Handwerck W. Christian Bertch X, Margaret Laugenor W
    Laugenhagen 562
    Laury 563
    Lautenshlaeger 292 746

407 LAWALL: Daniel, L Saucon, yeoman 23/3/1796-27/1/1797 Barbara w. ch Ludwig,
    Anna-Margaret the late w of Christopher Ketterman, Gertraut (w of George
    Seitz), Philip Bernina (w of Valentine Horn). Ludwig Mispickel X, and neph
    Daniel Beidelman X. John Stout, Henry Shaffer W
    Lawall 180 223 245 573 527 615
    Lawatsch 460
    Lawfer 152
    Lawrence 230

408 LAZARUS: *Martin, Allen twp 7/1797-20/7/1797 Leonora Lazarus X, George Ehret X.
    Casper Ritter, John Daniel Young W
    Lazarus 605
    Leadbetter 303

409 LEAN: *Michael, Easton, yeoman 13/3/1781-24/4/1784 Adam s. mens steps Michael
    Yohe and Mary his w. dau Margaret (w of Fredk Heegor). Robert Traill, George
    Ehrenfried W
    Lean 798

410 LEARN: John, L Smithfield 17/5/1777-27/10/1781 Catharina w X ch George X, Mary,
    Rachael, John, Jacob, Catharina, Rebecca, Andreas, Peter, Sarrah, Adam. George
    Philips W

411 LEDLIE: Andrew, Easton "Practitioner of Pysic" 8/1/1791-12/4/1796 mens "personal
    estate in Ireland and elsewhere in Europe": David Clymer and Robert Traill
    as X and Trustees for "old friend and housekeeper Elinore Hunt" natural s
    John Ledlie, alias John Butler ("least any should quible about names"), s of
    Bridget Butler. John Townes, Abraham Jones W Codical 31/10/1793-sis Isabella
    (w of Rev George Simpson, living near Armagh, N Ireland. John Mulhollan, J.
    Walton W. Affidavits of Jas. Hollinshead and Thomas McKeen Esqrs. "Wm Craig
    a fraudulent bankrupt of which proof in abundance are in my desk". Caveat
    filed by Samuel Bowman of Luzerne, Esq 26/1/1795, who states that his w Eleanor,
    the only dau of Wm Ledlie decd eldest bro of said Dr Andrew. Various sig-
    natures to docmts. Thomas B. Dick of Easton; Hon John Ruk; John Mulhollen:
    John Arndt: John Currie: George Ihrie: James Chestnor: John Ross: Abraham
    Horn: Samuel Sitgreaves: James Ralston: Daniel Stroud: Jeff. K. Heckman
    Peter Hollinshead
    Lehnert 264
    Leibert 15 183 746

412 LEIDIG: Leonard, Easton, cordwainer 21/4/1791-31/5/1791 Catherine w. ch incl
    George (minor) bil Jacob Arndt jr X and guar. Robert Traill, Conrad Ihrie,
    Jacob Michell W
    Leidy 412 416
    Leisering 200 418
    Leisor 361
    Leith 5 217

413 LEMBKE: Francis Christian, Nazareth, minister 16/8/1776-9/9/1785 Margareth
    Catharine W X ch John, Catherine-Elizabeth, Renatus, Christian-William. s of
    1st w Francis-Christian. J. Francis Oberlin of Bethm. merchant and John J.
    Jungberg of Nazareth, merchant co-X. Joseph Otto. Ferdinand Detmars, Melchoir
    Christ W
    Lembke 417 542 632

414 LENTZ: Conrad, Whitehall, yeoman 10/7/1801-10/8/1801 Saloma w X. ch George,
Catharina, Saloma, Conrad, Daniel, Steffen. mens lds of John Shuck, George
Samuel; Nicholas Klotz coK. John Samuel, Daniel Acker W
Leny 25

415 LERCH: Gratus, L Saucon 5/6/1794-9/10/1794 Anna-Maria w. ch Jacob X, Tobias X,
Maria, Appolona, Elizabeth, Catherine. mens 2 ch of s Philip, decd John and
Henry. Henry Ohl, Chas Hartman W

416 LERCH: Anthony, the elder, L Saucon, yeoman Margaret w. ch John (eldest) X,
Andrew X, (read Anthony X), Frederick, Peter, Margaret (w of Geo Emrich),
Elizabeth (w of John Leidy), Susanna. mens John Shymer s of dau Anna-Maria
decd. mens John, Anthony, Frederick, Peter, John, Margaret, Adam, Esther
and Samuel Beidelman. ch of my dau Catharine, late w of Adam Beidelman.
Frederick Laubach, Andreas Heller W also signed by Robert Traill. Anthony
Lerch
Lerch 4 6 43 65 241 352 354 371 394 472 493 627
Lesher 202
Lesser 527
Lessig 94
Leston 593
Levering 127 156 178 226 355 451 487 503 542 549 578 698 704
Levers 169

417 LEWIS: John, Salem, N. Car. "but now of Bethlehem" 17/11/1788-11/12/1788 Cath-
arine Elizabeth w X. bil William Lemnke X. mens Joseph Horsfield, Frederick
Kampman, John George
Lewis 294 421 439 738 758

418 LEYSENRINCK: Conrad, Whitehall 5/8/1781-(?) mens w. ch Conrad, John, Eve,
Andrew, Peter et al sil John Crob, sil Jacob Harman. Peter Kohler W
Lezgh 206
Lichtenwalter 462 637 706
Lichtenwiler 488
Lidweiler 215
Likena 282

419 LILLY: George (?)-2/4/1791 Nicholas Mittenberger, William Kromer W
Limbach 383 555 695 689 737
Limeberger 380
Lindenmeyer 785
Linder 120

420 LISCHER: John, Bethlehem twp 19/2/1774-15/5/1783 wife X. ch Mary, John, George,
Anna-Elizabeth, all minors. Jacob Loesch co-X and guar. Melchoir and Jacob
Christ W
Lister 445
Livegood 281
Lober 203
Lockerby 227 432 652
Loder 582

421 LOEFFLERN: Maria Dorothea 18/1/1786-6/6/1789 mens Herbenicha Dorothea, Johann-
Jacob and Johannes Wagner. Tudwig Renatus; Maria-Barbara Loeffler: Elizabeth
Lewis of Bethm. Anna von Marshall; Wilhelm and JohannaKSophia Schreyer;
Johann-Andreas Huebner; Andreas Dueppel: Hans Christian Schweinitz, Christian
Frdk Otto, Jacob Rubel W
Loeffler 421

422 LOESCH: *Herman, Bethlehem, miller 17/1/1789-4/5/1791 Mary Johanna w. ch
     John, Christina, Mary-Elizabeth: stepdau Rosina Beyer "now at Litiz,
     Lancaster Co". Peter Rickicker X. Tobias Boeckel X both of Bethm. John
     Hasse W. Codicil appts s John and sil Peter Jungmap hus of Christina X mens
     steps Fredk. Beyer
423 LOESCH: George, Gnadenthall, Bethm twp yeoman 30/11/1784-9/9/1790 ch Hermanus
     X, Christina (w of Christian Frederick of Salem, N.C.), Phillipina (Winland),
     Maria-Barbara (Smith), Jacob (decd mar Anna), John-Adam, Maria-Catherine,
     Balthasar, sil Valentine Fuehrer co-X William Edmonds, George Hartman W
424 LOESCH: Jacob, Nazareth, yeoman 21/2/1774-22/11/1782 Anna w X. ch John-
     Christian, John-Jacob, Anna-Philipina, Abraham, Susanna-Catherine-
     Elizabeth (youngest dau). b mens "patents to ld in North Carolina in hands
     of Jacob Blum": William Venables and Thomas Hugh, tenants on said land bro
     George Loesch and bil Jacob Blum and friend Jacob Bonn Esq of N. Car. X and
     guar for N. C/ part: bro Herman Loesch, co-X for Penna part. James Simonton,
     Henry Jacoby, Thomas *Ruckman, all of Mt Bethel, yeomen W William Edmonds
     affd. having written will
     Loesch 420 763 767 783
     Logan 102
425 LONG: *John, senior, Mt Bethel miller 24/2/73-8/12/1786 Mary w. 6 ch s and 6
     dau Elizabeth, Margaret, John, Catherine, Elias X, Mary, Joseph X, William,
     Jacob, Abrham, Sarah, Barbary. sil John Dietrich co-X. Henry Dildine, John
     Long, Michael-William Masterson W Codicil W by Hugh *Patterson and Benjamin
     Depue
     Long 560
     Loph 249
426 LORENTZ: George (?)-29/11/1789 Maria E. Lorentz X Francis Thomas X, William
     Boehler X. Jacob Fluckinger, George Flueckinger W
     Losh 242
     Louh 180
     Loventz 426
     Lowry 26
     Luckenbach 657 766
     Ludwig 206 516 648
     Lum 113
     Lumbach 169
     Lutts 365
427 LUTZ: Margaret ?/8/1791-5/12/1794 Benedict Lutz X Peter Seiler W
     Lutz 304 472
428 LYLE: Robert, Forks twp 28/10/1765-24/11/1766 wife X. Francis Thomas and
     ch Robert, John, Moses, David, Aaron, Jane, Elisabeth, Rosannah, Eleanor,
     Mary, bro John Lyle of New Brunswick N.J. and friend David Allen of Mt Bethel
     co-X. Thomas Sillyman, Mary Holmes and William Edmonds W
     Lyle 430 669
     Lyndenmeyer 302
     Lynn 371
429 McCALLUM: John, L Mt Bethel 12/9/1792-25/1/1793 Abigail w X. mens dau Elizabeth
     (Ayres) minor under 18 yrs: his bro Ephriam. Peter Simonton co-X bil John
     Oxford co-X. Rev Asa Dunham, William Richart, David Atres W. Codicil W by
     Daniel McCarter, Martin Oxford, John Oxford Sr
     McCarter 137 429
     McCarty 328 329

McCartney 469
McBurneu 499
McCalister 567
430 McCONNELL: William, Lehigh twp 27/6/1759-28/2/1760 Margaret w X. ch James,
William, Mary, Martha, Lydia, Margaret. Thomas Herron of Lehigh, David Allen
of Mt Bethel and Robert Lyle of Mt Bethel co-X. Mary *Perrey, Margd *Perrey
and Mary Perrey jr W
McConnel 282
431 McCRACKEN: Robert, Mt Bethel 24/12/1780-17/4/86 mens 3 dau having iss Anne (w of
Samuel Rea, decd), Margaret (w of John Vanetten), Jennet (w of John Neilson).
Samuel Rea and William McFarten Esq X. Peter Middagh, Moses Phenix and
William Rea W
McCracken 661
McEntyre 88
McFarren 440 441 533 626 660 708 758
432 McGINNES: *Edward, L Smithfield 7/9/1777-4/7/81 mens Robert s. "what was left
in care of Jacob Phillips of Clavenick". Mary Kress w of Christian Kress.
Sarah Lockerby w of Robert Lockerby. Christian Kress and Robert Lockerby X.
Abraham Van Campen, Moses Vancampen, Josiah Jennings W
McHenry 233
McIlhany 582
McKeen 411
McMichael 521
433 McNAIR: John, Allen twp 20/3/1762-2/3/1763. Christina w. ch William, John, Ann;
gdch Sarah and Christian Wilson. John Walker and James Craig X. Charles Wilson,
John Hays and William Hays W (read William Walker)
McNair 87 233 301 347 400 401 546 567 743
McNeill 74
Machlin 169 396
434 MACK: William. senior, Up Mt Bethel, yeoman 12/9/1793-25/1/1794 Anna w. mens
"late sil Herman Dildine decd, hus of Margaret". lds of William Mack s of John,
decd. dau Margaret Dildine and Mary Goodwin; gddau Anne and Mary and gds
George ch of George decd. gds Jacob Mack s of decd s John. gdch Jacob, John,
AAnne, George, Elizabeth and Mary ch of late John Mack John Scott, Esq of L Mt
Bethel, Mr Thomas Bar of Up Mt Bethel and gds William Mack jr X. Thos. Parry,
Henry Hartzell, Peter Beer W
Mack 15 48 86 372
435 MAGASH: Henry 7/6/1760-(?) Elizabeth w. sil Bernhard Feer, P. Braun, George
Arnold, Ph. Meyer W
Magee 499
Maisch 437
436 MAISTER: *Adam (?)-9/3/1798 Adam Heckman and Conrad Bachman W
Makes 250
Manderson 490
437 MANNI: Jacob, Williams twp carpenter 2/1/1764-10/6/1765 Anna Mary w. ch. mens
3 ch of s Jost, decd. friend Mathias Bruch X. Henry *Miller, John Moer, Johann-
George Maisch W
Manny 289
438 MANTZ: *Conrad, Lynn tsp widower 23/5/1774-13/11/1792 ch Jacob X, Barbara,
Magdalena, Philip Moser and John Stout of L. Saucon W
Marck 20 603
Marekel 573

Markel 292 676

Marks 67 469

439 MARSCHALL(von): *Anna Dorothea, Bethlehem ?/8/1795-23/2/1796 mens niece
Johanna-Elizabeth v Schweinitz X, neph Frederick Christian von Schweinitz:
Rosina Schulze: Wilhelm-Heinrich and Jacob van Vleck. Elizabeth Lewis.
Hans-Christian von Schweinitz co-X, Jacob van Vleck and Elizabeth Lewis W
Marshall 306 322 357 378 395 421 630 631 634 738 794

440 MARTIN: James, Mt Bethel 14/5/1767-16/7/1767 Ann w X. ch Joseph** Thomas**
James**, Isabella, Jane, Mary, Anna, Sarah, Eleanor. William McFarren, John
Ralston and Anthony Moon co-X, John Clark, Margaret Clark, J. Walker, J.
Horner W   **given land in Augusta Co. Virginia

441 MARTIN: Ann, widow of James 27/12/1798-16/12/01 mens above and gddau Ann Moore:
and ch of s Joseph (James and William). William McFarren X. Samuel Rea,
James Moore, Jeptha Anison W
Martin 95 129 307 479 480 563 591 675 714

442 MASON: William, Mt Bethel 25/1/1794-25/2/1794 Mary w X. ch Alexander X, Thomas,
Jannes (Reay), Elizabeth (Martin), Hannah, Mary, Hester, Martha. Ephriam
Simonton co-X. James Edmiston, Isaac Covert jr. William Hazlet W

443 MASON: *Francis, Mt Bethel 15/1/1790-29/5/1790 Esther w X. ch William X, Mary
(w of Peter Middagh), Henry, Martha (w of Wm. White). John Coningham, Robert
Galloway, Alexander Sillyman W

Masser 537

Master 436

Masterson 425

444 MATHIESON: Christian, Christian Spring, brewer 17/5/1790-6/7/1796 mens Samuel
Steip of Antigua Godholf Erdman: Hans Peterson; Hans-Christian v. Schweinitz.
George Golkowsky X. Johannes Schmall N. Weber

Mauer 81

Maulae 531

Mawberter 46

445 MAYER: John Philip, Nazareth, shoemaker 2/7/82-11/12/1782 mens bro Jacob Mayer
(who had eldest ch Philip-Jacob): friend Detlef Delfs: Wm. Bister mgr.
Single Mens Ho. George Golkowsky X. Francis Sciffert, Johann-Gottlieb Younf W

Mayer 235

Meckes 353

Meekly 123

446 MEINDER: Borekhard 7/15/8/1797 no Mentz, D Straup

447 MEISTER: *John 10/11/1752-15/6/1754 Sibilla W. ch Michael, John-Philip, John-
Henry, John-Jacob. George Schaumbach and Nicholas Stechler guar. Philip Diehl,
Adam Krames W

448 MELCHOIR: *George, Hamilton, farmer 2/5/1779-(read *George, Salisbury. 20/12/
1766-1/10/1767) Elizabeth Barbara w. ch Michael, Catharine (w of Leonard
Kessler). Christopher Wagner X. Bernhard Straub, Frederick Stuber W

449 MENEGAR: *George, Hamilton, farmer 2/5/1779-14/12/1779 ch John (eldest s),
Mary-Elizabeth, Mary Chatrine (mar), Chatrine (w of Christian House), Christina,
Elizabeth (w of Jacob Deatrick), Abraham, Christian X, Daniel X, Abraham
Miller, Laurence Kunkell W

450 MENNIG: Peter, Allen twp 6/4/1779-(?) Sibilla-Margaretha w X. ch minors. mens
"Reutenbusch Weister's Line". George Reutenbusch co-X

Merck 51 126 222 358 604

451 MERK: John, Bethlehem, clerk 29/6/1795-3/1/1797 "late dearly beloved w had by
    her 1st mar Joseph, Abraham, Anna-Maria, Johanna (w of Geo. Miller), and
    Elizabet Levering". mens Godch Maria-Susanna d of Abraham X and Anna Levering:
    Gods George s of Christian Ebert. Mary w of Anthony Smith. John Hasse,
    Anthony Smith W
452 MERKERT: Peter, Plainfield. Christina-Margreta w. ch Johann-George, Rosina,
    Christina.
453 MERSCH: David (?)-18/4/1798 George Merach X, Peter Laffer X. John Herman Reiss,
    Jacob Fahlstick.
454 MERSCH: Adam 19/4/1796-23/4/1796 John Dieter and Jacob Miller W
455 MERTZ: Henry, Rockland, Bucks 20/6/1786-31/3/1788 ch Philip X, Henry, William,
    John-Jacob, Catharina (w of Conrad Repp), John-George, George-Henry X, Maria
    (w of Peter Fink). Henry and Conrad Mertz W
    Mertzel 586
    Mertzler 212
456 MESSINGER: Elizabeth, Forks twp 8/5/1795-9/10/1795 ch mens Christian X, Michael,
    Peter, Charlotta (w of Conrad Shearer), Abraham, Margreda, Elizabeth (w of
    Philip Hickenboden), Mary, Cecilia. mens gddau Betsy, dau of Henry, Christian,
    Peter and George Butz, and Joseph Heller, John Hilgert and Philip Emrich. mens
    gds s of Conrad Sherer, named Jacob. mens Jacob Messinger. (The testatrix was
    the widow of Michael Butz q.v. 83) Michael Butz and Jacob Shoemaker W. The X
    renounced and letters were granted to John Hillyard. (see Everman's
    Genealogical Studies)
457 MESSINGER: Michael, Forks, yeoman 23/5/1791-10/11/1791 Elizabeth w. ch John
    (eldest s) X, Michael, Jacob), Catharine (w of Fredk Wilhelm), Mary (w of
    Peter Kocker), George, Daniel, Abraham, Elizabeth (w of George Stecker),
    Philip. mens lds of William Smith, John Brown, Cornelius Weigandt, Joseph Potts,
    John Arndt, Jacob Shoemaker, Jacob Able, William Bingham. bt ld of Edward
    Evans in 1764. lds of Nicholas Kemer, Andrew Ripple. Henry Albricht, John
    Youngberg and William Henry W
    Messinger 363 569
458 METZ: Peter, Plainfield 16/2/1767-16/4/1767 Elizabet w X. ch Valentine, Catherine
    Elizabeth, Hannah, Mary D., Conrad, Ever. Casper Dull co-X Thomas Clark W
459 METZGAR: *John, L Smithfield farmer 7/10/1794-11/11/1794 Elizabeth Catharine w
    X. mens ch Jonas, Catharina, Maria, Julia, Elizabeth, Susanna, Sarah, Maria
    (2d ment), Margreda, Sarah (2d ment), Annah. Woolly Houser co-X. Francis J.
    Smith, Jacob Transue, Adam Fuller W
    Metzgar 23 594
460 MEURER: Philip, Bethlehem, cordwainer 14/4/1760-1/7/1761 ch Christina, Magdalena,
    Salome, Elizabeth, Ann-Maria. Joseph Spangenberg, Matthew Hehl and And-Anton
    Lawatsch, all of Bethm X. Johan Muhler, J. Okely W
    Meusch 73 200 619
    Meuzen 133
461 MEYER: *Jacob 11/3/1790-24/1/1791 Henry Koch, Henry Roth W
462 MEYER: Nicholas, Macungie twp 8/12/1783-5/2/84 Magdalena w. ch Jacob X, Daniel,
    Susana, Catharina, Maria, Magdalena, Elizabeth, Ann-Margaret, Anna-Barbara.
    mens lds of John Lichtenwalner, Herman Mohr, Henry Geise, Melchoir Seip, John
    Fetter, John Knerr, Jacob Bare. John, Herman and Henry Mohr W
    Meyer 107 113 129 216 258 316 323 368 369 370 382 435 488 517 537 548 635 637
        674 675 714 784 791
    Michael 425 485 513 677 682
    Michler 1 23 29 598

Micke 598

Micksch 32

463 MIDDAGH: Peter, Mt Bethel 15/8/1778-28/10/1790 ch Garret X, Cathingie, Maritti, Elizabet, Anne, Peter X, Rebecca. gds Johannis (s of Anne). Andreas van Vliet co-X. Benjamin Depue, Adrian Aten, William Red W

464 MIDDAGH: Tunis, Up Smithfield, yeoman 2/2/1754-10/6/1771 Catherine w. mens ch Cornelius X, Elijah X, Elias X, John Vanaken, Wm. Ennes W

Middagh 3 4 431 443 463 661 758

Miess 484

Miksch 211

Mill 507

465 MILLER: *Conrad, Williams, potter 5/5/1790-3/6/1791 Barbara w X. sil Elias Transu. Abraham Miller, John Koplin, Stephen Krumrein W

466 MILLER: Christian, Moore twp yeoman 13/11/1784-27/11/1784 ch George, Anna-Maria Kaply), Anna-Margaret (Shaneberger), Maria-Fronica (Swartz), Catherine (Slaiger), Christian. sil Michael Swartz X. John Hugus, Andrew Kraft, Paul Nelig W

467 MILLER: John, Northampton 5/2/1785-19/2/1785. ch John of Halifax, N.S. Margaret (iss by former hus John and Mary Minter), mens 9 gdch by Elizabeth and John Ehrhard: Paul and Catharina Miller, ch of s Peter decd; Peter and Elizabeth Stimel, ch of dau Anna-Maria decd. Catharina and Mary Sheupt "being also ch of my said dau Margaret decd by her last hus George Sheupt". John Ehrhard X, Geo Graff X. Peter Hawk, Jacob Newhard, P. Rhoads W

468 MILLER: Verona, Bethlehem, wid of Jacob 11/1/80-3/9/1780 ch John of Newmanstown, Verona, spinster. bro Henry Frey of Litiz, carpenter X Geo. Huber, John Hasse, Phebe Payne W

469 MILLER: Alexander, Mt Bethel 15/2/1781-3/3/1781 w. ch Sarah, Samuel X, Matthew, Alexander, Thomas X. mens steps James McCartney: "wido" Jones: Margaret Bomand. John Ralston co-X. George Marks, Andrew Bowman W

470 MILLER: Henry, "heretofore citizen and printer of Phila. but now of Bethm" 27/9/1781-30/4/1782. mens Rev Geo Neisser, now of Yorktown, who had a decd bro Augustin Neisser, who has iss: William Edmonds of Nazareth who had sil Augustus Schlesser; Rev Nathaniel Seidel of Bethlehem: Hans-Ch. Schweinitz: Rev Jacob Freus of Bethm. Rev Daniel Syderick and W f Gertrerit: neph John Henry Mueller, schoolmaster and ld surveyor at Gundelbach, Maulbrunnen, in Dukedom of Wurtembg. Mr Peter Miller, serivener of Phila. Worshipful William Henry of Lancaster X, William Edmonds, Esq of Nazareth X. G. Young, George W

471 MILLER: *John, L Mt Bethel, yeoman 12/2/1791-11/9/1799 mens Agnes. ch of neph Samuel Miller, Alexander, John, Matthew, Samuel, Sarah, Mary. ch of his niece Martha Miller, Thomas, Elizabeth, Isabel. neph Alexander Miller of New Bruns- wick X. James Thompson, Adam Teel, And. Miller W

472 MILLER: Bernhard, Williams, yeoman 4/12/1792-12/1/1793. Eva w. ch Henry X, Jacob, Frederick, Barbara (w of Paul Brod iss), 3 ch Henry-Valentine, John- Jacob, Frederick; Barbara (w of Wm. Gruver) Elizabeth (w of Jno Odenwelder), Eve (w of Balzer Eckert). sil John Odenwelder co-X. Benedict Lutz, Anthony Lerch jr W

473 MILLER: Christopher, Macungie, yeoman 7/10/1788-14/11/1788. Ottila w X. ch Valentine, Lawrence, George X, Maria-Magdalena, Elizabeth, Maria-Agata. gdch Catherine Hettler. John Fogel, Andrew and John Miller W

474 MILLER: Leonard (?)-30/6/1788 John Morh X. Jacob Eckel, Adam Karb, Lewis *Klotz W

475 MILLER: Christian, Forks, farmer 26/1/1789-9/4/1789 Catherine w. ch Isaac, Abraham, Frederick, John X, Jacob. mens sil George Bittenbender: John Shnyder, Deeter Sickman. Robert Traill, Christopher Bittenbender W. mens lds of

475 MILLER: contd. Andrew Grotz, John Shynder, William Sharlock
476 MILLER: Alexander, Plainfield 14/10/1773-18/11/1773 "his mother" ch Thomas,
    Elizabeth, Isabel all minors. bro Samuel Miller and bil Alexander Miller X,
    Alexander Calbreath, Joseph Gaston, John Culbreath W
477 MILLER: Jacob, yeoman 14/3/1777-10/10/1777 Elizabeth w X. ch Henry, and 4 sis.
    Conrad Eary coX Thomas Sillyman, J. Repscher, Peter Irig W
478 MILLER: *Jacob senior, Up Milford, husbandman. 25/11/1778-7/2/1780 Anna Barbara
    w ch Mathias of Phila, Magdalena (w of Andrew Gerstenberger), Dewald (decd had
    4 ch). mens gdch Jacob and Barbara Miller, ch of 2d s Michael, John Kystand
    X. Jacob Huber, Jacob Witner W
479 MILLER: Sanders, Bedminster twp 20/2/1765-28/10/1765 Mary w. ch John, Jean
    (Thompson), William, Noleye (Wilson), Elizabeth, Oliver. James Martin of
    Bucks X. Robert Robinson X. Daniel Bibighause, James Miller W
480 MILLER: Mary, Mt Bethel 10/12/1765-8/8/1766 ch James, Agnes (Moore). Wm. Moore,
    J. Martin W
481 MILLER: Erhard, Moore twp 25/1/1766-15/10/1766 Anna Ursula w X. ch Erhard,
    Elizabeth. Christian Spengler, George Golkowsky W
482 MILLER: William, Mt Bethel 13/8/1767-10/12/1767 Jean w. Thomas, Robert, Joseph,
    William. bros Alexander and Samuel X. Alexander Calbreath, Joseph Gaston,
    Thomas Miller W
483 MILLER: Albright, Plainfield, yeoman 21/6/1762-3/9/1762 Eve w. ch Dorothy (Frank),
    Henry X, Henickel, Adam. 2 s, Henry and Nicholas X Dul Bower, Thomas Clark,
    Hannicle Snyder W
    Miller 6 13 17 23 25 31 36 43 105 108 134 146 203 244 195 200 253 261 274 300 325
           334 372 437 449 451 454 460 533 540 554 583 611 612 615 636 647 688 758 770
    Miltenberger 170
484 MIESS: *Anthon, Whitehall 15/2/1780-(?) Margareth w. "I declare her unwise, she
    having eloped from me near one year, her Expectancy or share is to remain in the
    hands of my executors to be kept to supply her wants" 5 ch. Stephen Schnyder
    and Peter Steinberger. Lorentz Neuhart, Valentine Steiner, Fredk *Neuhart W
    Minegar 203
485 MICHAEL: Adam, Northampton, laborer 6/3/1777-28/8/1783 Elizabeth w and ch of
    Jacob Dersum of Up Saucon X. Peter Rhoads, Elizabeth *Hessner Lawrence Hauck W
486 MINSTER: Paul, Bethlehem 15/2/1783-1/12/1792 Barbara w X. mens Tobias Boeckel
    (perhaps w's 1st hus)M stepch George-Frederick, Tobias, Christian: Elizabeth
    Boeckel: Anna Rauschenberger: Rosina Rose: Mary Beck: Ch-Fredk Oerter of
    Bethm. clerk and Hans-Ch von Schweinitz of Bethm. gent X. Christian R.
    Heckenwelder, Jacob Ruebel, John Hasse W
    Minster 231
    Minter 467
    Mispickel 407
    Mitchell 412 581
    Mitsch 549
    Mittenberger 419
    Mixdorf 231
    Mixsell 739
487 MOEHRING: Michael, Nazareth 8/3/1796-16/6/1796 Elizabeth w X. William Horsfield
    and Jacob Christ co-X. Jos Levering, Fredk Shoefer W
    Moehring 114 254 503
    Moffet 499 536
488 MOHR: Harman, Macungie 17/3/1777-(?) Susanna w X. ch Frederick X, Jacob X, Nicklas
    Harman, John. Johann Lichtenwalter, Nicholas Meyer W

Mohr 53 216 295 316 462 474 726
Mohrdick 783
Moll 372 669
Montango 732
Moody 101 533
Moon 440
Moor 130 360 437 668 701
489 MOORE: John, Mt Bethel 30/1/1778-2/3/1778 ch William, Mary, Anthony, Jean,
    Frances. mens Thomas Moore and James Thompson as bros. William and James
    Moore W
Moore 58 100 101 231 441 661 708
490 MORDEN: James (6 lines) 12/4/1758-(?)
Moreland 209
Morey 47
491 MORGAN: Evan, Hamilton twp 7/3/1777-23/4/1777 Sarah w X. ch Elizabeth, Esther,
    Hanna, Even, John, Luies, Thomas; Col. Jacob Stroud X. Nicholas Depui, Joseph
    Smith, Simeon Cady W
Morgan 396
Morhart 127
492 MORITZ: Henry, Williams twp yeoman 9/11/1795-18/11/1795 Rosina w. ch Elizabeth
    (w of Matthias Hetterer), Christina (w of Philip Clouss), Wilhelmina (w of
    Adam Fly), Anna-Mary (w of Geo. Knecht). sil G. Knecht X. John Spangenberger
    and Bernhart Spangenberg W
Moritz 404 663
493 MORREY: Jacob, Up Saucon 5/7/1775-5/3/1793 ch William X, Peter X, Jacob, Susanna-
    Catharine (w of John Wind), Sabela-Christina (w of John Lerch), Rupina. Baltzer
    Buchecker and Gotthard Morry X.W. Codicil incl Mary-Eve w
Morrey 76 643
Morris 20
494 MORRISON: Andrew, L Saucon 9/3/1761-29/9 1761 mens Hannah: Nathaniel s of Andrew:
    Andrew s Cornelius Cane: Hannah Cane: Thomas s of Abraham Versislow and
    Susanna. John Riggs and Andrew Orstroem W
495 MOSER: Peter, Forks, yeoman 19/6/1780-19/8/80 Eve w. ch Michael, George-Adam,
    Andrew, Jacob, Paul-Tobias, Peter, John, Eve, Catharine, Magdalene. Wm. Raub
    and Philip Odenwelder X. John Spangenberg, John Jaeger, John Odenwelder W
496 MOSER: *Tobias. senior. Lowhill twp yeoman 9/12/1800-29/12/1800 Magdalene w.
    ch Tobias, Daniel, Catharina, Elizabeth, Christina, Margaret, Anna-Maria, and
    Lydia Dormeyer dau of my dau Barbara, Michael Beiber jr and John Moser X Peter
    Gross, John Moser W. mens "stepp daughter"
Moser 191 361 438 738
Mott 46
Metz 704
Mower 203
497 MOYER: *George, senior, Bethlehem twp yeoman 30/1/1792-26/3/1792 Margaret w X.
    ch George X, Ann-Mary, Magdalene, John, Susanna. Joseph Jones, Johan Schweit-
    zer, Michael Kocher W
498 MOYER: *John, Lynn twp weaver 2/11/1781-22/1/(read 2/11/1761-22/1/1762): Mary
    w. ch Andrew, Rachael. mens steps John Moyer: lds of Joseph Holder. Charles
    and Andrew Foulk of Lynn X. J. Everitt, S. *Percher W
Moyer 270 791
Muckly 60 697
Muecke 32 254
Muenster 302 630 632
Muhling 321

499 MULHOLLEN: Jane, Nazareth twp 28/11/1799-1/8/1800 mens Mary McBurney: Thomas
McBurney's dau Sarah: "if my bro John should have a dau called Jane, if not
to his dau Elizabeth"; bro William's dau Christian: John Hunter's dau Jane
and Mary: sis Sarah Magee and her dau Rebecca Magee: "if bro Daniel should
have a dau called Jane, if not to his dau Mary" bro Daniel's youngest dau:
bro William's w Sarah: Thomas McBurney's s: sis Elizabeth Hunder: Nancy
Agnew: Mary Wilson: Elizabeth Manderson: sis Sarah Magee: Hannah Dawson:
bro Daniel's w Isabella. Bro John Mulhollen and James McBurney X. Lettice
Ralston, Maria Ree, Mary Moffer W
Mulhollen 411 499 536 534 554 647 739 782
Mullen 720 727
Mundy 291
Murry 678

500 MUSGENUNG: Jacob, Whitehall, blacksmith 7/6/1798-4/12/1798 mens sons Jacob and
David and their sis Dorothea, Christina et al. gddau Salome Swartz and Cath-
erine Swartz. sil Peter Rhodes, friend Godfried Knauss X. Johannes Roth,
Peter Rhoads, Eve *Roth W

501 MUSSELMAN: Jacob, Allen twp yeoman 18/2/1784-4/12/1798 (read -31/12/1784) Mary
w. ch Christian, Chaterine, Elizabeth, John, Jacob, Barbara, Peter, Joseph,
Susanna, Fronica, Margareth, Rudolph Kauffman X. Ulrich Shoemaker, Geo *Diechy W

502 MUSSELMAN: John, Up Saucon 4/1/1773-29/3/1773 Elizabeth w. Jacob, Veronica,
Catherine, Elizabeth. Jacob Yoder, John Newcomer jr. X. Melchaer Knaepple,
Philip Buchecker W
Musselman 25 200 259
Myer 107

503 MYRTETUS: Christopher Gireon, Nazareth 1/1/1795-29/3/1799 Elizabeth w X. ch
Elizabeth (Rutter), Christopher, John, Jacob Christ of Nazareth coX and Trustee.
Michael Moehring, Joseph Levering W John Youngberg J. P.

504 NAGEL: Frederick William, Moore twp yeoman 22/11/1779-22/12/1779 Anna Mary w. ch
John-George X, Frederick, Christian, steps Henry Ribbert. sil Henry Kleppinger
co-X. John Kleppinger, William Kromer W
Nagel 28 134 354 643 686
Neale 139

505 NEFF: Bernhart, Heidelberg twp 7/5/1778-? w X. Bernhard minor s. Henry Neff co-X
506 NEFF: Ulrich, Heidelberg twp 23/12/1773-(?) Elizabeth w X. ch Conrad X, at al.
Bernhard *Neff, Henry Reinhart* W.
507 NEFF: Ulrich, (?)-27/12/1799 Conrad Neff X. Christian Kram, Simon Crantz W
Neff 236
Nehlig 369
Neighbert 231

508 NEIHART: Frederick, Whitehall 1/1/1766-14/5/1766 Maria Margaretta w. ch Freder-
ick, Lawrence, Peter, Christopher, Daniel, Juliana (w of Stephen Schneider of
Whitehall), Salome, Elizabeth-Barbara, Sophia; George Knauss, George-Jacob
Kerm W
Neihart 571

509 NEILE: Henry, Whitehall 16/12/1773-6/6/1774 Maria-Barbara w X. appts John Hunsicker of Heidelberg, guar of s Paul and Henry. and Dewalt Kendil, Peter Kendel
as guar of dau Margaret, Eve and Catharina. Conrad Shnyder, David Sasn and
Danile Shnyder W

510 NEISER: Joseph (?)-14/5/1794 Hans-Christian von Schweinitz X. Jos Horsfield,
Jno Wasser, J Hasse
Neilson 431

Neisser 470
Nelig 456
Nelsen 663
Neuhart 484 508
Newbaye 618
Newcomer 64 81 502
511 NEWHART: *George, Allen twp yeoman 18/6/1787-25/3/1800 ch George, Margaret (w of
    William Daniel), Frederick, Daniel, Juliana, Catharine, Elizabeth, Christian,
    John, Philip, s John X. Peter Rhoads, George Graff, Stephen Snyder W
    Newhard 123 330 333 467 610
Newman 145
Newton 282
Neymeyer 84
512 NITSHMAN: Immanuel, Bethlehem (?)-20/1/1791 Mary w X. Jacob van Vleck X. Rev
    Johan-Andreas Huebner, Dr Eberhard Freitag W
    Nitschman 632 734
Nombauer 155
513 NOWLANE: John, Bethlehem, yeoman 5/6/1776-25/8/1777 Gertrude w X. dau Christina
    (w of Henry Hertzel of Allen), Elizabeth (w of Henry Wm. Laval of Bethm), Cath-
    arina (w of Jacob Weigand of Forks), Anna-Martha (w of Frederick Beyer of
    Bethm). steps Nicholas Michael of Bethm. Jacob Weigand and J. Okely W
    Noy 758
514 NUNGESSOR: George, Lynn twp Eve w. ch Martin, Peter. Ann-Eve w X. and her bro
    Fredk Romich X. Nich Hermany, J. Volck W 17/12/1759-16/10/1762
    Nungessor 343 673
515 OBERDING: Ann, Up Milford. widow 22/3/1760-24/6/1773 Penna. Hospital X. Mathias
    Ox, Adam Shuller, Lewis Klotz W
    Oberfields 227
516 OBERLY: *Rudolph, L Saucon, yeoman 25/12/1779-1/4/1780 Margareth w X. ch Eliza-
    beth, John X, Anthony, Jacob (minor), Christian. mens ld given Rudolph O. in
    L Saucon patent 3/1/1755 and 1/7/1765. John Ludwig, Frederick Laubach and
    Handitor Heller W
    Oberly 65 204 315 365 405 413 728
    Obershimer 94 293 580 687
    Ochs 515
517 OCKER: *John Michael 27/1/1755-13/5/1760 w and ch incl Nicholas. Nicholas Mayer,
    Nicholas Fisher W
518 ODENWELDER: Philip, senior, Forks, yeoman Chatarind w. ch Philip, Michael, John,
    Catharina, Ann-Mary, Elizabeth, Rosina. Michael Kreiter co-X Peter Seip,
    Thomas Hartman W
    Odenwelder 83 472 495 744 788
519 OERTER: Christian Frederick, Bethlehem, clerk. Anna decd w. ch Joseph X, Catha-
    rina, John Schropp, Abraham Andreas, Christian R. Heckenweler
    Oerter 29 264 309 412 486 574 630 631
    Ogden 318
    Ohl 4 315 371 415 727 756 757 790
    Okely 76 79 121 164 297 303 328 329 362 363 364 370 405 460 513 525 529 585 618
        620 734
520 OLLENDORFF: Charles, Forks 27/4/1768-5/4/1768(?) mens Stephel, Henrich, Ludwig,
    Mathias, Barbara and Melchior X Stecher. William, Margaret and John Edmonds

Ollenwein 573
Omenseter 166
Opp 180 186 360 587 703 739 755
Ord 31 213
Orr 328 329 794

521 ORSTROM: Andrew, Salisbury 29/5/1788-9/10/1790 Christn w X. Stephanus Tool co-X
Peter Rhoads, John Rosmus of Salisbury, yeoman W.
Orstroem 136 494 657

522 ORT: John, Up Milford, yeoman 11/11/1797-18/4/1798 Mary Rosina w X. 10 ch incl
Jacob (youngest) John Moritz of Up Milford co-X J. Vogt, Adam Schuller W

523 ORT: *John, Up Milford, yeoman 29/4/1785-7/5/1789. ch Henry, Christina (w of
Geo Ringer), Margaret (w of Jacob Zerfink), Catharina (w of Jacob Kalver),
Eve (w of Geo Fleckinger X), John, Barbara (w of John Koch), John Brobst, G.
Krubel W
Osterlein 345
Osterlie 760
Ostrong 720
Oswald 543 544 583 637 780

524 OTTO: John Matthew, physician, Bethlehem 28/12/1785-19/8/1786 ch John-Matthew,
Rebecca, Sophia-Magdalene. Francis Thomas and William Boehler, wheelright of
Bethm X. mens ch of his bro Thomas Otto and his sis Eve Catherine Kechin, and
also the ch of Joseph Otto of Nazareth. Gods Christian Fredk Kock of Newwerd,
Germany. Francis Thomas, guar of Sophia-Magdalene. Tobias Boeckel, Peter
Vettertive W

525 OTTO: John Frederick, Nazareth 24/7/1766-5/2/1780 Judith w. Joseph s X. bro
John Matthew Otto of Bethm X. William Boehler, J. Stein, J. Okely
Otto 8 104 162 164 302 338 339 413 539 600 632 765

526 OWEN: David, Up Saucon, yeoman 17/3/1791-10/5/91 Margaret w X. ch Elizabeth,
Hannah, Solomon, David. bil Wm. Grothouse X, Abraham Seider X. Christian
Clymer, Conrad Brinker W Abraham Sellers W to renuncn. of X of will

527 OWEN: Jane, Up Saucon, widow 13/11/1773-7/5/1783 sil Marget Thomas. mens Jane
Cline: Elizabeth Chilcot: Sarah Owen jr. James Samuels: sis Margaret
Rhoads; Ellen Shoemaker. Thomas Foulke of Richland, Bucks X. Abraham Syder,
Eleanor Samuel, Elijah *3. Lesser W

528 OWEN: *Sarah, Up Saucon, wid of David. 13/8/1791-28/4/1792 mens 3 gdch Owen,
Hannah and Sarah O. ch of s Thomas decd. Nathan s X. sil Jonathan Scott X.
Henrich Scheffer, John Stout W

529 OWEN: David, Up Saucon, yeoman 26/7/1786-29/6/1790 Sarah w X. ch David, Joseph,
Jonathan, Nathan, Lydia, Sarah (w of Jonathan Scot of Up Milford coX), Rachael
(w of Samuel Bachman), Mary (w of Wm. Grothouse), Abigail (w of Jacob Ziegler-
fuss). mens Sarah, Owen and Hannah dau of s Thomas decd; ld of in L Saucon
and Salisbury: lds of Ehrhart Weaver, Geo Hall, Matthias Egner, Michael
Zeisler and David Smith. J Okely, Geo Hall, Christopher Hansel W

530 OWEN: Thomas, Up Saucon, yeoman 22/6/1764-6/9/1773 Jane w X. bro David Owen:
sis Margaret Thomas. Martin Steinmetz, Christopher Hansel, Jacob Geisinger W

531 OWEN: Thomas, Up Saucon, yeoman 20/12/1782-24/3/1783 Margaret w X. ch Owen,
Hannah and a ch "yet unborn". bro David Owen jr co-X. Jaques Maulae, John
George Maulae W
Owen 136
Owens 375
Ox 515
Oxford 429

Oytnine* 678

Palmer 74 113 152 170 403 644 782

632 PARIS: John Fernando N Exemplification of Will dated Surrey street, in the Strand, in the Parish of St Clement Danes, in the couty of Middlesex, gentleman 7/1/1748. confirmation of will 18/12/1759 (v. 229). mens The Archbishop of Canterbury: sisil Mrs Elizabeth Gough

Parry 26 86 434 667

Parsens 615

Patten 269

533 PATTERSON: *Isabel "at present the wif of Hugh Patterson of L Mt Bethel, and late wid of David Allen 28/2/1800-27/5/1800 mens Elizabeth dau of Alexander Miller, late of Plainfield: cous Elizabeth Finney wid: cous Isabel and Martha, dau of Alexander Miller: John, William, Samuel, Jane and Margaret the ch of William McFarren; the ch of Samuel Rea: 3 ch of sis Mary Falhever wid.: Rev Asa Dunham: neph Alexander Miller Sr. cous Elizabeth Bowman: neph Alexander Miller X Samuel Rea, Robert and Adam Moody W

Patterson 22 58 389 425

Paul 752

Payne 79 468

Pearson 566

Peeter 143

534 PEIFFER: Christian, Easton, yeoman 19/2/1785-3/3/1785 Catherine (pres w). John, minor s by pres w: 6 ch by 1st w. mens dau Chaterine (iss) John Deichman of Easton X. Robt Traill, Conrad Ihrie jr W

Peissel 123

Pell 22

Pember 639

Penkerton 178

Penrose 268

Peppard 25

535 PEREY: James, Bethlehem twp farmer 26/9/1757-25/4/1759 Mary w. ch Mary, Margaret, Martha, William. Jas Ralston, Jno Hutchinson, Jean*Herron

Perrey 430

536 PERRY: *Mary, Bethlehem, wid. 30/7/1783-16/10/83 mens ch James X, Mathew, Lucy; neph Samuel Fulston minor. William Barlay co-X. William Moffet, Jacob Dech, John Mulhollen W

Peter 313 294

Peterson 32 444

Petri 380

537 PETTER: Jacob, Heidelberg 20/6/1777-(?) Elizabeth w X. Peter Meyer X. mens John Ulrich Petter, soldier, oldest s had Elizabeth: mens decd dau Mary-Magdalena Masser and 2 ch: mens sons Philip-Jacob, Nicholas, John-Jacob, Abraham (minor). sils J John Baer, John Adam Baer, Peter Shop and Adam German. Henry Geiger, C. Reidy W

538 PETTER: Rudolph, Heidelberg 9/2/1777-(?) Susanna w X. mens s William: lds of John-George Blass, Lorence Wehr, Michael Gruenewalt, Henry Geiger, John Hunsucker co-X

Petter 709

Petty 39

Peyser 744

539 PFEIFFER: Peter, Plainfield, yeoman 1/5/1796-15/11/1797 s George (w Elizabeth). Mils Tillison, and William Henry X. Joseph Otto, Melchier Christ, Joachim Weigman W

540 PFEIFFER: *George, Plainfield 4/9/1800-23/5/1800 Catharine w. Dietrich Bauer X.
James Hall and Andrew Miller W
Pfeiffer 385 534 747
Phenix 97 431
541 PHILIPS: *George, L Mt Bethel, yeoman 16/5/1800-(?) Catharine w X. mens Mary
Hacock: mens bros and sis: Abraham Ball co-X. John Kempfer, James Dingman,
George Reichart W
Phillips 133 410 432
Pierch (?) 632
Pierson 653
542 PITSCHMAN: George, Bethlehem 26/1/1786-6/6/1789 mens Elizabeth M. Pitschman.
Abraham Andreas X Abraham Levering, William Lembke W
Polliard 509
Porcer 498
Potts 457
Pretz 762
Prevost 22
Price 587 702
543 PROBST: George, Lynn twp 20/11/1795-12/12/1795 (died 21/11) Jacob Oswald, Jacob
*Wannemacher W
544 PROBST: Mathias, Lynn twp (?)-15/1/1793 mens Michael, Samuel and Daniel Probst
X. Jacob Oswald and Philip Hess W
Probst 40 45 68 72 551 694 695 699 771
Quick 227
Quier 718
Rabenalt 671
Rainsey 108
545 RALSTON: Samuel, Allen twp farmer 30/8/1785-4/1/1786 ch Mary, James, Samuel,
Gabriel (s), Sarah, Isaac, Letea. bro John Ralston X, Robt. Brown X. Jas
Lattimore, Jean Rosbrug, Jno White W
546 RALSTON: John, Allen farmer 29/12/1794-24/2/1795 Christina w. ch James X, Mary,
Lettice, Ann, Jean, John, Christiana, Robert, Samuel. sil Jas Lattimore co-X.
Hugh Horner, John Brown W. mens John McNair Sr
Ralston 73 88 93 233 347 411 440 469 499 535 581
Ramaly 697
Ramstaine 62
Rasmus 570
Rath 394
Ratzel 286
Rau 366
547 RAUB: George, Williams, yeoman 6/12/1780-3/2/81 mens w and ch Andru, William,
Barbara, Dorethe, Margrete. bil Christian Eacker: lds of Fredk. Klinhans,
Michael Raub. (V)fallenteen (B)beitelman X. Michael and Christian Raub W
Raub 495 708 707
Rauch 5 312
Raup 275 611
Rausberg 188 (burg)
Rauschenberger 52 488 718
Raymond 324
Rea 431 441 533 660 758
Reay 442
548 REBER: Adam 8/6/1790-30/12/1794. Mary Reber and Geo Meyer X. Nicholas Rummae,
Henry Fatzinger W

Rebsher 133
Reckas 613
Reckert 656
Red 463

549 REDER: Henry, Bethlehem twp yeoman 28/2/1788-4/9/1801 Anna Maria w. ch John-
George X, Conrad, Elizabet (w of Abraham Sorver), Peter X, Ludwig-Henry
(decd had Anna-Maria, Margaret, Henry), Julianna (w of Jacob Shick). had ld in
Moore twp. George Golkowsky, Christian Mitsch, Joseph Levering W. Jonas
Hartzell read will

Redwick 180
Ree 499

550 REEDER: (read REEGER): Frederick, Easton, dyer 17/4/1780-13/5/1780 Barbara w.
ch Frederick, Jacob, Anna-Margareth. Jacob Grotz and Abraham Labar X. John
Spangenberg, Andrew Kachlein, and Abraham Horn W

Reeger 409
Reese 192
Reiber 107
Reich 71 127 222 359
Reichard 721
Reichel 55 222
Reichenbacher 107

551 REICHERD: Ludwig, Weissenberg twp 24/7/1777-(?) ch George X, Margareth (iss),
Catherine (iss), and ch of dau Catherine-Elizabeth decd. sil John Gackenbach
co-X. Michael *Brobst, Joseph Seefried jr, Mathias Probst W

552 REICHERT: George, L Saucon, yeoman 5/4/1787-2/10/1787 Eve-Sellomy w. ch Michael,
Andrew, John, George X, Jacob, Geo-William, Magdalena (w of Andrew Zegenfuse)
iss), Mary-Barbara, Elizabeth, Catherine. T.*Cally, Peter Sean, Math.
Schneider

Reichert 215 356 429 541 761
Reidy 647
Reil 554

553 REIMEL: *Jacob, Sr. Up Mt Bethel, yeoman 6/3/1794-22/11/1796 Sarah w. ch John,
William, Mary, Caty, George, Elizabeth, Jacob. John and Philip Weidman X.
Peter Anderson, Peter Labar W

554 REIMER: Valentine, Williams, yeoman 30/3/1793-31/3/1794 Margareth w X. ch Isaac,
Daniel, Jacob, Henry, Margareth 2w of John Reil X, Elizabeth (w of Peter
Unangst), Catharine (w of Peter Lantz) Sarah (w of Jacob Miller), Anne-
Barbara, Anne-Eve, and ch of dau Susanna decd, Christian and Peter Holland.
Caveat by Isaac 31/3/1794 N Court of John Mulhollen, David Wagener, judges:
John Arndt, Reg. John Spangenberg, Daniel Reinheimer, Christian Best, Abraham
Transue, Valentine Miller W

Reimer 586

555 REINARD: Christian, Up Milford, yeoman 7/9/1784-12/10/1784 Chaterine w. ch
John X, Jacob X, Christian, Martin, Catherine, Mary-Elizabeth. Henry
*Hertzell Sr Frederick Limbach Sr and William Schoeffler W

556 REINEKE: Abraham, Bethlehem 16/9/1758-1/7/1761 Abraham s. Joseph ("otherwise")
Augustus-Gottleib Spangenberg and Peter P(B)oehler, both of Bethm. clerks,
guar. J. Okely X John-Martin Kalberhahn, Nicholas Henry Everhart A Shontz W

557 REINHARD: *Henry, Penn twp 31/5/1794-15/12/1794 Elizabeth w. sil David Wyant
X. Boaz Walton and Jesse Walton W

558 REINHARD: George, Up Saucon 29/10/1778-11/12/78 Anna w X. bros Abraham, Henry,
Andreas. John Stahl, Casper Rungfeld W

559 REINHARD: Peter, Up Saucon, yeoman 4/5/1762-4/6/1762 Gloria w. mens bros and
sis. bro George X. Peter Knapply Balzer Kokal A. Wind W

Reinhard 24 325 505
Reinheimer 304 554
Reiner 211
Reiss 167 261 317 453 615 737 770

560 REISWIG: Margaret (?)-10/4/1790 Goerge Horner X Geo Klein X. Peter Long, George
Kneibel W

561 REISWIG: John, Up Milford, cordwainer 30/7/1787-17/11/1787 Margaret w. ch John,
Peter, Conrad, Elizabeth (w of Geo Sam and ch John and Regina Sam), Susanna
(w of George Hoerner). Geo Klein X. Geo Kreibel X. Jacob Erbach Jacob
Schmitt W
Reitzenbach 8
Reiz 701

562 REMELY: Michael (?)-16/1/1793 Geo Remely X Lewis Eneke, Peter A Laugenberger,
William Kern W

563 REMELY: George, Whitehall, bauermann 30/9/1800-29/10/1800 Elizabeth w. ch
Ambrosius X Johanes, Elizabeth, Barbara, Jacob, Maria, Heinrich, Magdalena,
George, Peter; Peter ROTH co-X, Fredk MARTING, A TROXELL, J STREIN W

Renatus 421

564 RENBURY,Michael, Moore twp yeoman 14/5/1770-31/7/1773 wf. ch John, Michael,
Philip-Henry, Maricha, Elizabeth. Yeast Trashback (Dreisbach) of Lehigh and
Philip Drum of Morre X. William Carruthers, Paul Flick, Frederick Beck W
Rennel 297
Rentzheimer 123 240 570
Repp 455
Repscher 477
Rese 251
Reser 223
Resh 361
Ressner 485
Rex 608 662 751
Rhoads 16 23 48 53 72 103 140 225 234 278 330 333 372 373 374 467 485 500 511 527
592 610 669 724 748 751
Rhoan 753
Ribbert 504

565 RICE: John, Macungie, shoemaker 6/3/1770-1/4/1771. Regina w X. ch George X,
Frederick, Louweese, Regena, Christina. Francis Wesgo co-X, Ludwig Stahler,
Ludwig Stahler, Ludwig Larush W
Rice 95 163 177 578
Richards 198 668
Richardson 593

566 RICHTER: *George, Exeter twp Berks 3/12/1754-10/11/1756 Kertrout w. dau Anna-
Margaretta (w of Peter Ingoldt). steps George Hoffman, minor. Stephen Shoe-
maker, Adam Bowman, Thomas and Benjamin Pearson W
Richter 186
Rick 289
Ricksecker 422

567 RIDDLE: John, Allen twp 10/10/1769-29/8/1769 Jane w. ch John, William, Dana;
Mary, Jennet, Sarah, Susanna, and a dau (w of Peter Brady). James Craig,
Arthur Lattimore and James McCalister, John McNair W
Riedy 537
Riegel 766 774

568 REISER: Ulrich, Up Milford, yeoman 23/4/1784-27/9/1784 ch John, Casper (3d s),

568 REISER* contd. Elizabeth, Andrew, John-William, Anna-Barbara (w of Fredk. Depp),
     Mary (w of Peter Shuler), sil Frank Delp (iss). ds of John Dirr, John Youd.
     George Krible), Baltzer Krauss, Hannes Weber W ·
     Rieser 300 689
     Riess 84
     Riggs 494
     Righter 277
     Ringle 103 193
     Ringer 523 563
     Rinker 330 372
569 RIPPLE: Nicholas, Easton, yeoman 2/1/1777-16/6/1777 Margaret w. ch Casper,
     Elizabeth (w of Philip Koch iss), Mary, Andrew, Michael, Peter, Catharine et al.
     lds of Harman Shnyder, Peter Coacher, Michael Messinger. Abraham Labar and
     Herman Shnyder X. Johannes Deichman, Robert Traill and John Batt W
     Ripple 457 654
     Rishel 292 753
     Risurg 247
570 RITTER: Henry, Salisbury 16/6/1789-23/1/1797 John Rasmus and Catharine Rentzh-
     heimer W
571 RITTER: Andrew (?)-26/4/1790 Michael and Peter Nyhart X. Jacob Strein, Asa
     Simons W
572 RITTER: Casper, Sr Bethlehem twp yeoman 26/1/1791-2/4/1792 Maria w X. ch Casper
     X, Michael, Daniel, John, Elizabeth (Gilbert), Susanna (Deitel), Barbara
     (Balliet). gdch Maria and Casper Kleckner, Barbara and Susanna Balliett.
     Daniel Ritter, Johannes Duebler W
     Ritter 170 333 408 779
     Riveland 213
573 ROAD: *Catharina, Macungie 10/8/1761-22/9/1761 dau Catharina Marekel. mens Yost
     Ollenwein and wf. Peter Haas, Melchoir Hermany W
     Robinson 479
     Roehrig 293
     Roesli 159
     Roeter 681
     Rogers 209
574 ROHLEDER: *Martin, Nazareth twp (?)-5/5/1797 Anthony Smith, Abrhm Andrews. Joseph
     Oerter W
     Robt 238
575 ROMELY: John Gottfried (?)-26/7/1799 John Schropp X. John Hasse, George Fetter,
     Daniel Kleist W
576 ROMICH: *Frederick, Macungie 19/?/1783-(?) ch John, Joseph, Adam guar·X. Henry
     and daus. Nicholas Harmany W
577 ROMICH: *Henry 25/6/1786-1/7/1786 Andrew Giering X. Henry Knauss and George
     Christ W
     Romich 197 367 368 514 590 595 742 777
578 ROMIG: Adam, Up Saucon, miller 17/4/1797-2/10/1798 Elizabeth w. ch John X,
     Samuel, John-Adam X, Jacob, Daniel, Peter and daus. mens lds of George Bauman,
     Peter Werst, Jacob Keck. Owen Rice, Abraham Levering, John Hasse W
     Romig 320 591 725 740 761
579 ROMIG: Frederic, Macungie 25/8/1800-10/11/1800 w. s John. bil Peter Walberth
     X. Henry Romig, Frederick Walberth W
580 ROOFFNER: Philip, Moore twp 4/6/1784-7/10/1784 Eve w. X. ch Simon, Anna, Mary,
     Henry, Anton, Philip, Anna-Margrat. "his w s Joseph". Peter Obershimer co-X.
     Jesse Jones, Nich. Shell W

581 ROSBRUG: John, Allen twp 19/12/1776-(?) Jean w X decd bros s Robert and John
Rosbrug. Rev Mr Alexander Mitchell, and Mr John Ralston co-X, John Walker,
William Carruthers W
Rosbrug 269 282 545
Rose 52 486
Rosenkraus 733
Rosmus 128 521
582 ROSS: Thomas Sr L Mt Bethel 5/7/1796-11/1/1798 Jane w. ch David X, James X,
Thomas, Elizabeth, Zacheriah, Mary. John Johnson, Samuel Rothrock, William
Loder, James McElheeny jr W
583 ROSS: Charles (?)-22/1/1800 Hannah w X. Jacob Oswald co-X. Adam Kunkle, Adam
Miller W
Ross 95 324 357 663
584 ROTH: Nicholas, Moore twp 3/6/1777-12/6/1777 Susanna w X. ch Barbara, Margareth.
Andrew Diemer co-X. Martin Meyer, John Schuyler W
585 ROTH: Jacob, Lehigh, yeoman 6/9/1775-11/12/1788 Anna Maria w. bro Daniel Roth,
Baltimore Md. (iss). Bernard Kuntz of Lehigh co-X. Adam von Erd, J. Okely,
William Boehler W
Roth 270 461 500 563 638 711

586 ROTHENBURGER: Nicholas, farmer 26/12/1781-(?) ch Jacob X, Elizabeth, Adam,
George, John-Peter. Philip Hertzog co-X. Christ *Reimer, H.S. Mertzell W
587 ROTHROCK: John, L Saucon, yeoman 26/8/1790-22/4/1794 Mary w. ch Michael,
Margaret (w of Peter Zug), Mary (w of Isaac Price), Ann (w of Daniel Price),
Asmath (w of David Shelly), John, Jacob, David X, Abraham, Catherine(decd
and iss), Isaac X, Samuel, Joseph. Daniel Price co-X. Jacob Arndt, Jacob
Opp, Robert Traill, John Young W Renun. of David X. John Beyl, Geo Rothrock W
Rothrock 23 263 376 582
Rouchenberger 109
Roup 36 385 654 681 788
Routenbush 450
Rub 103
Rubrecht 771
Ruch 628
588 RUCK: Michael, Christian spring, Bethlehem twp 30/3/1783-19/5/1797 Maria
Christina w X. ch Anna-Elizabeth, Johanna-Maria. George Golkowsky co-X.
John Hanke, Henrich Beck W
Ruchman 424 782
Rudolph 752
Ruebel 35 306 357 421 426 486 636
Reutcher 597
Rummae 548
589 RUFF: *Sebastian, Up Saucon, yeoman 28/5/1801-10/10/1801. Susanna w. ch
George X, Valentine X, Christina (wid of Martin Mush), Magdalena (w of Henry
Schatz). Adam Kortz, Michael Flexer W
Ruffner 374
Rumel 760
Rumfeldt 774
Rumfield 64 172
Rummel 760
Rungfield 558
Rundio 170
Rup 270

Rupp 27
Ruprecht 45
Rush 411
Russi 43

590 RUTH: *Philip ?/7/1783-11/10/1783 Michael Schneyder X, Daniel Schwartz X.
Valentine Schaeffer, J. Romich W

591 RUTH: Mary Elizabeth, Macungie, wid. 13/9/1800-11/11/1800 ch Susanna (w of Abraham Romig), Elizabeth (w of Joseph Heyman), Magdalena (w of David Dauckel),
Peter, Sallie, bro Daniel Swartz X. Samuel Swartz, Jacob Martin W

Rutter 503

592 SAEGER: Christina, Whitehall, yeoman 17/2/1790-11/2/1801 Mary Susanna w. ch
Nicholas X, Jacob X, Daniel, Magdalena, Catherine, Barbara, Christina,
Margaret. George and Peter Rhoads W   SAEGERS 642

Sam 561

593 Samuel: Isaac, Up Saucon, yeoman 8/1/1781-26/5/1781 Eleanor w X. mens "bro
Thomas-Eleanor s bro": 2 ch William and Samuel and dau Jane. ld of John
Erehart. John Thomas X, Samuel Foulke X, John Leston, John *Richardson W

Samuel 414 527

594 SAND: *Adam, Forks, farmer 29/12/1792-6/3/1793 Elizabeth-Christina w X. sons
Adam X, Michael, John. lds of Andrew Kachlein. George Sewitz, Robert Traill
W. Codicil Andrew Metzgar and Christian Correll W

Sands 148
Santee 328 329
Sasn 509
Sassamanhausen 784
Savitz 53
Saylor 385
Schaeffer 19 41 81 150 187 218 237 246 308 321 407 487 528 555 590 644 701 737 801

595 SCHANCKWEILER: Jacob, Macungie (?)-20/8/1787 s Jacob X. Jno Heinkle Sr John
Remich W

Schanckweiler 641
Schantz 381
Schatz 383
Schaumbach 447
Scheetz 676
Scheibele 336
Scheidt 246
Scheilli 230
Scheive 179

596 SCHELPP: Peter, Allen twp (?)-26/2/1788 Christian Schelpp and John Arndt X

Schenk 263 265
Scherre 753

597 SCHEUEREMAN: George, Up Milford 5/2/1777-(?) Catharina w. ch Theobold, Elizabeth
Elias-Barbara. Michael Schindel and George Stitzelmeyer both of Lancaster X.
J. Jost Wentz, Samuel Ruetscher W

598 SCHIERGER: *John, Christianbrun, Bethm twp 24/?/1785-30/7/1785 mens bros, sis
living in Europe sis Maria Michler in Litiz: inheritance from bro Andrew of
Europe: bond of Godfrey Belling: cous Catherina Mickin, her hus Mathias, and
their s John Micke: bonds of Michael Hern, Henry Beck and Jos Schweushaup:
Geo Golkowsky. Christian-Fredk Steinman cous X. Saml Steip, J-Geo Weiss W

Schindel 597
Schlayer 61

Schlebach 19

599 SCHLEPPY: Hans Ulrich, Bethlehem twp 22/7/1789-10/8/1789 Julianna w. ch Jacob, Daniel, Eve, John, Conrad, Michael. gddau Susanna. Conrad Kocher, John Clauss X. Jacob Eyerly jr Conrad *Kocher, John Clauss W

Schlicher 218

600 SCHLOESSER: August, Nazareth 11/2/1795-14/2/95 mens sis Judith, dau of John Edmonds: Margaret Schloessern dau id Mathias Schloesser. Jacob Eyerly Jr. Conrad* Joseph Otto, Melchior Christ W

601 SCHLOESSER: August, Nazareth 11/8/1790-13/7/93 mens bro Mathias of Christiansfiel Danish Hollstein: bil John Edmonds and his dau Mary: cous Maria Faneberg of Herrnhoth. Margaret w X William Henry, Joachim Wigman, both of Nazareth

Schloesser 8 109 162 339 470

Schmayer 777

Schmeier 367

Schmetzer 262

602 SCHMEYER: *Jacob, Macungie, yeoman 14/4/1791-28/4/1791 Waltborga w. ch Jacob, Susanna, Crate, Regena, John, Daniel, Anna-Elizabeth, Philip X. bro Peter Smoyer co-X. Nich Klotz, Michael Kahn W

603 SCHMIDT: Melchoir, Macungie, husbandman 5/3/1796-9/8/1796 Mary w X. ch Melchoir X, Margareth (w of John Marck), John, Jeremiah and Adam Smitt, John Kane. George Steininger and Peter Smith W

604 SCHMIDT: Anton Sr. Bethlehem. 12/3/1793-4/5/1793 s Anton X. Abraham Boemper. Francis Thomas and John Merck W

Schmidt 2 32 222 231 (see Smith)

605 SCHMIT: Peter, Allen twp yeoman 10/2/1771-25/3/1771 Anna-Barbara w ch mens Jacob, Henry, Catharine (w of Geo Hagencuch). mens steps Martin Lazarus: Peter Funck: lds adj Geo-Henry Hertzel, Peter Kockert. neighb Geo-Henry Hertzel, Nicholas Sterner X Mathias Shoener, Peter Kockert W

Schmitter 13

Schmoyer 602

606 SCHNELL: John George, Nazareth, weaver 1/8/1781-8/1/1783 Anna Helena X. ch John, Elizabeth, Christian-Fredk (minors). friend Jacob Christ of Nazareth hatter X. John Dealing, Henrich Brunner, John Hasse W

607 SCHNABEL: George, Bethlehem twp yeoman 4/2/1800-12/5/1800 ch Jacob X, Matthias X, Andrew, Catharine, George, Elizabeth, Mathias Gress and John Schneider W

608 SCHNEIDER: Balser (?)-15/4/1800 George Rex and Christian Bloss W

609 SCHNEIDER: Jacob (?)-24/4/1800 Casper Engler and Ludwig Spoonheimer W

610 SCHNEIDER: Stephen, Whitehall 14/3/1796-9/5/96 4 s Frederick, Henry, Peter X, Daniel X. 3 dau incl Magdalene Hall. Peter Rhoads and Laurence Newhard W

611 SCHNEIDER: John, Forks, yeoman 25/7/1791-2/9/96 Elizabeth Catherine w. ch John, Christina (w of Mathias Stacher), Catherine (w of Geo Hillman), Elizabeth (w of Christopher Raup), Susanna (w of John Kocher), Jacob X, John-George, Peter, David. sil George Heilman co-X. Andrew Gretz, Detrict Seckman, Abraham Miller W

612 SCHNEIDER: Adam, L Saucon (?)-5/4/1801 John Schneider X, Godfrey Miller X. Michael Heller, Jacob Kaufman, John Stumpf W

613 SCHNEIDER: John Peter, Lynn twp 25/4/1775-(?) Catherine X w. ch incl Lewis; Frederick Secher X, Henry Rickas, Philip Setler W

614 SCHNEIDER: Daniel, Whitehall 25/7/1778-(?) Dorathea w X. ch Daniel X, Jacob et al Conrad Shnyder, Peter Burkhalter W

Schneider 2 133 (see Snyder)

Schnerr 19

615 SCHOLL: Frederick ?/7/1754-25/4/1754 ?. Mary-Barbara w. mens Frederick and
Nicholas Scholl; Tobias (?): Siebella Lawall. Will adst. "to the care of
Mrs Grace Parsons, Mrs Edmund Woolley, at Up. end of 2d st. Phila. pr John
Wayell"

Schnyder 80 207 (see Snyder)

Schoen 240 349

Schoenlein 439 634

Scholl 207

Schonby 618

Schontz 556

School 286

616 SCHOONOVEN: *Redolphus, L Smithfield, yeoman 29/10/1752-21/12/1756 Dorothy w X.
2 ch. John Wood, Manuel Gonsales, James Hyndshaw W

Schoonover 96 732

617 SCHOOP: Martin, Weissenberg twp 15/5/1777-1/2/1777 Anna w. ch Eve, Barbara,
Fronica, Peter, (is) Jacob *Bachman, J. Horner, J. Helber W

Schoop 249

Schortz 220

Schreiber 373

Schreyer 421

Schriber 121 122 796

Schroeder 46

Schroff 116

Schropp 222 359 519 575 632 773

618 SCHUCK: John, Williams 4/7/1763-29/12/1767 Anna-Maria w. ch Mari-Catherina (w of
Henry Eiger), Rosina (w of Francis Newhaye), George, Dorothea (wid of John
Youndt), Christina (w of William Full bucht of Williams). Christopher Bitten-
bender X, Jacob Best X. Andreas Schonby, Andreas Brocksch, J Okely W

Schuck 181

619 SCHUG: John Peter, Forks, yeoman 28/12/1786-25/8/1794 Mary w. ch Christian, Adam,
Henry et al Abraham Mensch of Allen co-X. Mathias Stecher, Henry Stecker W

Schuller 84 189 522

620 SCHULPP: Peter, Allen twp yeoman 10/5/1780-18/4/1782 ch Peter X, Barbara (w of
Nicholas Fuchs of Bethlehem twp). A Boemper, John Okely, Andreas Shober,
Eterd Coordsen W

621 SCHULPP: Peter, Allen twp yeoman 6/10/1787-26/2/1788 Chrtina w. ch Elizabeth,
Peter, Conrad, Catherine et al. John Arndt X guar. John-Nicholas Fuchs,
Stephen Koehler, John Erhard W

622 SCHULTZ: Jacob, Plainfield 6/10/1792-8/10/1793 Barbara w. 1 ch Mary (minor).
Melchoir Christ X, George Claewell, John Steiner W

Schultz 439 738

623 SCHUMACHER: Rev Daniel, Weissenberg ?/4/1787-4/6/1787 Jacob (s?) X. Andrew
Buchman W

Schunenbruch 374

624 SCHUPP: Henry, Chestnuthill twp 27/3/1780-(?) w. ch Abraham X, Philip X, Frederick, Anna-Maria, Peter, Elizabeth, Adam Correll, Adam Sorver W

** Schupp 147   Schurger 598
** Schuraer 598   Schwab 281

625 SCHWARTZ: *George, Moore twp 16/2/1786-29/10/87 Maria Christina w. ch Michael
X, Anna-Margaret (2 ch Madelena, Christina), Adam, Philip, Geo. Barbara.
Paul Flick W

Schwartz 2 13 127 306 308 580 590

Schweinitz 55 195 222 231 421 439 444 470 486 510 632 634 738
Schweishaupt 32 224 598
** Schweitzer 204 497   Sciffert 445
626 SCOTT: John, Esq L Mt Bethel 22/2/1798-21/6/99 Anna w. ch William, George,
    Robert, Alexander X, Jane, Mary, Sarah. mens wf's 2 dau Ann, Catherine.
    William McFarren co-X & Benjamin Butler, Wm(?) McGarren, John *Snyder W
** Scott 434 520 529 683   Sealy 257
   Scull 319
627 SEBASTIAN: Michael, Allen twp yeoman 3/7/1780-12/12/1780 dau Regina (w of Conrad
    Kreider) ld in Fredk. twp Phila (adj ld of Henry Boyer, Nicholas Keston,
    Mardin Kuchle, Mathias Geist et al. s George Muhill (prob Michael). gdch
    Elizabeth Grider, John Lerch, R. Hays P Knauss
628 SEEGER: Samuel, Whitehall (?)-23/8/1789 Michael Seeger and Geo F Knauss X. ch
    Seeger Lor Ruch W
   Seem 552
   Seffel 195
629 SEGER: John Nicholas, Whitehall 22/10/1753-3/2/1762 ch Samuel, Christian, John
    (aet 21:27:11-1763) Anna-Mary (Shnyder), Anna-Barbara (Traxell) Christina-
    Barbara, Mary-Margareth, John-Nicholas, John-Jacob, Anna-Elisabeth. mens lds
    of Peter Traxler, Ulrich Burkhalter, John Shad, Michael Traxler. Philip Seger,
    John Nicholas Snyder W
630 SEIDEL: Rev Nathaniel Codicil to No 631 14/9/70 Anna Johanna w. John Ettwein and
    Paul Muenster, both of Bethm. clerks X. mens lds in Penna. N.J. N.C., West
    Indies. mens Fredk Marshall of Salem N.C. gentleman. Amadeus-Paulinus Thrane,
    Andreas Weber, John Fromelt, John Bonn, Christian-Frederick Oerter W
   Secher 613
   Seegal 195
631 SEIDEL: Nathaniel, Bethlehem, clerk. 20/6/1770-1/6/1782 Estate to friend
    Frederick Marshall of Salem, N.C. (see 630: same W except Fromelt)
632 SEIDEL: Anna Johanna, Nazareth, wid of Nathaniel 25/2/1788-6/3/1788 mens Peter
    Minster X, Hans-Ch. von Schweinitz X. bros Daniel and Christian Piesch of
    Germany: sis Dorothea Antony (had ch Anna-Dorothea): hus Nathaniel: John-
    Gottfried Seidel s of my hus sis now residing in Germany: Hannah Seidel dau of
    Gottlieb, bro of my lare hus Nathaniel: cous Anna-Dorothea Netschman N,
    Paul Minster: Anna-Johanna Hussey: Catherine Lembke of Widow's House. John
    Schropp, gentleman and Joseph Otto, Physician, both of Nazareth W
   Seidel 52 162 231 386 395 470
633 SEIDELL: Melcher 13/5/1771-(?) Margaretta w X. ch Peter, Magdalena, Margaretha,
    Catharina. John Huntzecker, Henry Geiger W
   Seider 76 169 526
   Seidlitz 231
634 SEIDNER: *Margaretha Barbara 7/23/2/1796 mens Wilhelm Boehler of Beth X. Margaret
    and Rachael Schoenlein of Litiz: Anna von Marschall. John George G. Weiss,
    Hans-Ch von Schweinitz, Verona Schneider W
635 SEIFERT: Peter, Lynn twp farmer 16/3/1766-31/5/1768 mens sil Jacob Weitzell X.
    sil George Breusch: Susanna, housewife: 3 sil Gerhard Schellenberger and
    Maria-Christina, his w: Jacob Weitzell and Susanna-Catharina his w: George
    Bruesch and Maria-Katharina his w. Valentine Brobst, Mathias Probst. Dewald
    Meyer W
636 SEIFFERT: Franz, Nazareth 21/9/1790-27/7/1795 mens bro Anton in Gnadenfreg: bro
    John in Rudelsdorf, Silesia: sis Theresa in Groshammersdorf, Saxony: and her
    hus John-Fredk Jones: friend Detlef Delfs: Jacob Rubel. George Golkowsky,
    Henry Miller, Joseph Stotz and Franz Seiffert W. also mens Verona Fisher of

636 SEIFFERT: contd. Neusahtz, Silesia
    Seiffert 195 635
    Seiger 697
    Seiler 427 653
637 SEIP: Melchoir, Macungie 26/12/1796-25/2/1797 Anna Regina w. ch John X, Peter X,
    Elizabeth, Catherine, Eve, Margaret, Magdalena. Maria-Eve, John-George,
    Catharine, George-Adam. mens lds of Conrad Keck, John Oswald, Geo Shuppert,
    John Lichtenwalter, John-Peter Geiss, Peter Haff and Jacob Meyer (all in
    Macungie): lds in Penn twp of Michael Habbis and Jacob Wannemacher. fil
    Henry Geiss. Jacob Horner, John Oswald and Conrad Kock W
    Seip 31 170 216 6 462 518 784
    Seitz 186 407
    Sellers 526
    Semel 414
638 SENGLY: Martin, Lehigh twp 9/4/1777-(?) Cornelia w X. ch George et al. Conrad
    Shnyder, Jacob Roth, Frederick Kuntz W
639 SERFAS: Philip, Chestnut Hill twp yeoman 11/3/85-20/3/1787 ch John, Jules
    (mar Pember and had Christian), Mary, William, Sarah, Frederick, Molly,
    Christian. mens fath and moth. ld of Adam Souer: Lewis Stecher Esq Justice.
    William Serfas, Adam Sorver W
    Serfass 147 258 712
    Settler 613
    Sewitz 252 594 674
    Seyder 752 753
    Shabel 607
    Shablie 267
    Shaeffer 51 (see Schaeffer)
640 SHAERER: *Valentine, Williams, Yeoman 23/4/1793-10/10/1797 Barbara w. ch. Adam
    X, Philip, Anna-Barbara (w of John Transue). mens ch of his steps John Vogt:
    lds of Francis Hillyard, Mathias Bruch, John Heller. Jacob Arndt and George
    Knecht W
641 SHAD (T): Henry, Macungie 14/3/1765-30/2/1768 Susanna w. had iss. mens "gdch
    Henry Shadt's s: Henry Brobst: Rosina Shadt's s": Henry Shadt jr bil Nich-
    olas Hermany X. George Steininger X. M Michael-George Edelman, Jacob Schank-
    miller W
642 SHADT: John 24/2/1777-(?) Elizabeth Catherine w. ch George, John, "2 youngest
    dau" Catharina (mar Bertih ? iss); mens 2 bros John and George: "to build
    barn like Samuel Saeger's". Charles Seeger, Charles Sheiveler W trans by
    Stephena Bolliet
643 SHAFER: George Sr. Salisbury 17/4/1800-22/12/00 Eva w. ch George et al. Samuel
    Geissinger and Wm Moorey X. Danil Diehl, ch. Nagle W
    Shafer 106 116 119 801 (see Schaeffer)
    Shaler 398
644 SHALL: Andrew, Moore twp 8/1/1801-2/2/1801 Anna-Elizabeth w X. ch Andrew X,
    Michael, Peter, Anna-Maria, Anna-Margaretha (w of John Dieter), Anna-Elizabeth
    (w pf Peter Shafer). George Palmer and Peter Shafer W
645 SHALL: Nicholas, Bethlehem twp 26/8/1772-18/11/1772 w. ch Michael X, Andrew,
    Nicholas, Anna-Mary. Thomas Hartman, John Frederick W
    Shane 53
    Shaneberger 466
    Shank 720
    Shankweiler 212

646 SHANTZ: *John (?)-29/6/1801 Abraham and Jacob Shantz X. Philip Walter, Ulrich
          Daster W
      Shantz 646
      Shantzenbach 691
      Sharlock 475
      Sharpe 60 234
      Sharry 679
      Shaw 209 250
      Shaerer 456

647 SHECKLER: Frederick (?)-7/6/1794 Frederick s X filed caveat 22/4/1794: pres at
          court; John Mulhollen, David Wagener, John Arndt, Daniel Stroud, Samuel
          Sitgreaves: Jacob Reidy and Jacob Miller W mens 647's w and dau Elizabeth

YRI SHEECK: *Valentine 29/4/1763-20/8/1763 ch Michael Christian, Ann-Mary
          (Trellinger), George, Gertraut (Holtz). George-Chas Ludwig (servant). Martin
          Buchman, John Ehrenhard, Jost George W

649 SHEIBLE: Michael, Up Milford 12/6/1770-1/8/1770 Barbara w. ch Martin X, Marg-
          aret, Barbara (decd), had iss Elizabeth, George, Bernhart Wensch co-X.
          Sebastian Truckenmiller, Jacob Holtzhauser, Rudolph Weiss W
      Sheible 279
      Sheiveler 642
      Shellenberger 635
      Shellhammer 78
      Shelly 587
      Shoeneberger 658
      Sherrer 640
      Shertzer 718
      Shick 549 719

650 SHICKLY: George, Williams, yeoman 24/3/1782-6/7/1783 Anna Maria w. George
          eldest s X. John Best, Philip Wettring W
      Shimel 791
      Shimer 232 262 384 727
      Shimier 667
      Shimp 672
      Shitz 715
      Shleppy 729
      Shlough 201
      Shluffer 107
      Shmayer 131
      Shneider 89
      Shnepf 467
      Shnyder 30 191 (see Snyder: Schneider)
      Shober 620 651 729

651 SHOBER: Andrew (?)-21/7/1792 Hedwig-Regina Shober X. John Hasse W

652 SHOEMAKER: Daniel, L Smithfield 2/2/1773-3/6/1773 Anna w X. ch Henry, Hannah
          (Emmens), Ann, Sarah, Samuel. Wonsfred, Elizabeth and Mary van Campen,
          daus of Moses Depue s of Samuel Depue X, Robert Lockerby, Benjamin Shoe-
          maker, Jas Brink W

653 SHOEMAKER: Michael, Williams 17/6/1780-(?) Mary-Chatarine w. ch Jacob, Peter,
          Conrad, Isaac, Abraham, Margareth, Elizabeth. Henry Bierson and Peter
          Seiler W
      Shoemaker 44 83 143 167 456 457 527 707 744
      Shoewalter 501
      Shoener 323 605

Sholl 580 662
Shop 537
Shonk 204

654 SHOUP: Ludwig Sr, Forks, joiner 6/12/1796-25/2/97 Christina w X. ch Catherine, Henry, Conrad, Lewis, Elizabeth, John, Susanna. sil Jacob Kachlein, Easton co-X Peter Ihrie, Wm. Roup W

655 SHOUSE: Frederick, Easton, mason. 18/2/1788-17/3/1788 ch Mary (w of Michael Yohe), Christiana (w of ?), Henry, Jacob, John. gds John Shouse. sil Michael Yohe X. Peter Shnyder, Robert Traill, Michael Traxell W

656 SHOUT: John, Up Milford 14/2/1785-6/5/1785 Elizabeth w. George, Catherine, John, Laua (w of Geo Kach), Michael, Magdalena (w of Adam Reckort), Adam, George, Eve (w of Thomas Ward). Andrew Engelman and Frederick Whiteman X Geo Wierman W

Shrawder 731
Shreiber 123 124 125
Shrigly 46
Shriver 54
Shropp 254 309
Shuck 133 414 716
Shuler 352 515 565
Shull 136
Shuppert 637

657 SHUETZ: Christopher, Salisbury 21/2/1763-12/8/71 Anna-Dorothy w X. ch 2 s and Anna-Dornotia. A. Luckenbach, Andreas Oestrom W

658 SHWARTZ: Michael, Moore, farmer 24/11/1801-17/12/1801 Fronea w. ch Peter X, Margrat (w of Peter Beckey), Susanna, Gegene (w of Henry Esch), Michael, Catherine (w of Christian Shoeneberger). Peter Beckey co-X. Abraham Kreider, ,ich Esch W

Shweishoupt 178
Shymer 416
Shynder 77

659 SICHER: *Jacob, Up Milford (?)-1/8/1792 John-Jacob Sicher X, Henry Wetzell X. Conrad Wetzell and Davis Strauss W

Sickman 277 475 611
Sieberling 299
Siebring 668
Sieder 193
Siegal 83
Siegel 1
Sieger 379 775
Siegfried 354 551
Siegler 529
Sietzelberger 296
Sill 726

660 SILLIMAN: Agnes, Forks 25/4/1774-20/2/1778 ch Alexander, John (mar had Thomas), Thomas; mens gddau Agnes Silliman: dauil Sarah (iss): George Bennet's note: 3 gds Thomas, Alexander and James Silliman. Samuel Rea, John McFarren X. John Lyle, Robert Lyle, Mary McFarren W

661 SILLYMAN: Alexander, Mt Bethel 1/6/1773-1/12/73 Margaret w X. ch Thomas, Isabella, David (under 14 yrs.). John Moore, Gerad Middach and James Beard co-X. Thomas and Robert McCracken W

Sillyman 58 428 443 477

662 SIMON: Lawrence, Heidelberg 2/1/1757-5/6/1758 Barbara w. ch Laurence, Catherine

622 SIMON: contd. (w of Christ Zimmermann), Elizabeth-Margaret, Elizabeth (w of
Peter Sholl), Elizabeth-Catherine (w of William Bricious), Margaret-
Barbara. Jacob Rex X, John-Leonard Fuhr X. George Rex, Jacob Bender, Philip
Feedler, John-Dietrich Baldauff W translated by John-Nicholas Snyder

663 SIMONTON: *Robert, Mt Bethel 21/7/1782-27/1/1786 Mary w. ch Epheraim, Robert,
Peter, Benjamin, Margarit (Nelson), Jean (Bretton), Easter (Ross), Thomas Ross
X, James Beard X. Thomas Ross, Benjamin Depue, Henry Jacobu W

Simons 571
Simonton 429 424 442
Simpson 411
Sipperlin 83
Siser 17
Sitgreaves 411 647
Sitler 45
Slaiger 45
Slaterony 213
Sleider 81
Sloomaker 566
Slough 722
Slye 678

664 SMITH: *Melchoir, Macungie 8/12/1784-9/8/1785. Margreta w. ch John X, Melchoir,
Jeremiah, Margaret(Baere); lds of Adam and Baltzer Smith, Jacob Kechly, Christs.
Stedler, Christian Dabler, Mathias Ripple. John Fogel, William Smith, Jacob
Horner W. mens also s Peter

665 SMITH: Abraham, Chestnuthill twp 4/7/1785-9/8/85 Nicholas Altimus, John Smith
and Adam Correll X, Sofel Christman, N. Correll, C Getz W

666 SMITH: Adam (?)-15/1/1800 John and Maria-Barbara Smith X. George Hantz, Peter
Schmidt W

667 SMITH: Richard, Mt Bethel, cordwainer 13/11/1787-3/4/1797 Elizabeth w X. ch
John, Catherine (Gillman), Amos X, James, Margaret (Shimier), Mary, Jane, Sarah,
Jerushe. Thomas Farry, Casper *Engler, Daniel *Devere, Geo *Labar, Elias
Dietrich W

668 SMITH: Henry, Mt Bethel ?/11/1786-22/4/1793 Margaret w X. ch John X, Jennet (w
of Philip Templar), Anna(siebring), Catherine (Richards ch Henry), gdch
William, Mary, Margaret Richard. James Depue, Sarah and Benj Depue W. renumtn
of X, Wit by David Moer and John Siebring

669 SMITH: *Ursula, Northampton, widow 14/8/1801-10/11/1801 ch George X, Michael X,
Eva (w of John Arnold), Melchoir, Joseph (iss), John (iss). John Moll,
George Rhoads W

670 SMITH: Rudolph, Salisbury 1/3/1777-23/7/1778 Barbara w. ch Jacob, Anna, Catharina, Rudolph, Daniel. Jacob Spinner, Henry Kech W

671 SMITH: John, Lowhill twp 19/11/1779-(?) weaver. Gertraut w. ch Ludwig X, Daniel,
Mary, Elizabeth, Magdalena, John, William, Henry, Casper. mens bt. ld of
Fredk Habernalt. J Horner, Michl. Diebler W

672 SMITH: Nicholas, Lynn twp 19/4/1766-26/7/1766 Catherine w X. ch Daniel, John,
Catherine, Jacob. Thos Everett coX. William Shrimp, George Herman W

673 SMITH: Jacob, L Smithfield 8/8/1761-25/4/1769 Magdalena w X. ch Johannes,
Michael, Abraham, "them 3 of my s not obeid me". Fredk-Wm. Catharina, Eliz-
abeth. Steven Horn, "overseer of will" Frederick Nungessor, Jacob Crotz,
Nicholas Shnyder W

674 SMITH: *Christian, Up Saucon 21/1/1756-11/6/1757 Ana w X. ch Jacob, Elizabeth,
Catherine, Anna. Trustees John Joeder jr Jacob Meyer. Henry Kooken and
Jacob Zevitz W

675 SMITH:* Nicholas, Lowhill 23/5/1757-11/6/1757 ch John-George X, John-David,
    Maria-Elisabeth (Makin) Dill-Bauer, Barbara (Mayer), Anna, Lisa Catharina
    (Wind). Maria-Margareth w. Jacob Klotz, and John-George Sieger W

676 SMITH: Michael, Up Milford 18/4/1780-10/5/1784 Anna Barbara w. ch John, Jacob,
    Daniel, Michael, Frederick, Elizabet-Margaret (w of Philip Scheetz), Eliza-
    beth (w of John Oytnine), Catherine (w of John Markle). Michael Ziegler W
    Smith 28 34 51 72 117 127 133 149 153 171 187 183 189 210 227 239 271 335 342
          346 392 393 423 451 457 459 491 529 561 571 574 603 604 605 687 689 728
          732 749 756 757
    Smell 372

677 SMYTH: Bernhard, Macungie 6/11/1767-1/12/1767 Anna Margaret w X. ch George,
    Adam, Margaret, Phillipena. bro Melchoir X and guar. Philip-Jacob Michael
    guar. P. Trexler, Danl Knauss W
    Sneider 66 214 (see Snyder et al)

678 SNELL: *Adam, L Smithfield 13/5/1782-7/8/1788 ch Mathias, Modelane(w of Patrick
    White), Catharine (w of David Williams), Susanna (w of Cornelius Vanflerd).
    mens stepdau Margaret Murry. Jacob Stroud X, Michael Slye X. John Fish,
    John Huston and William Courtright W
    Snell 203
    Snider 174

679 SNYDER: David, Up Saucon, yeoman 22/8/1785-1/10/1785 Esther w. ch Jacob, Catherine
    John et al. neighbors Abraham Snyder, John Geissinger and Philip Sharry Z.
    William Grothouse W

680 SNYDER: John, 26/2/1782-(?) Margaret w. 4 ch incl Frederick
    Snyder 34 152 221 222 256 270 281 326 335 396 439 475 479 483 508 509 511 552
          569 584 590 607 610 626 629 634 638 655 662 673 693 697 709 710 717 762
          796

681 SOAN: Peter (killed by indians) "nuncupative" (?)-16/5/1757 mar Anna Maria dau
    of Michael Roup. "Philip Peter Tipper and Anna Catherine" his wf "swore that
    they were present at the house of Peter Soan in L Plainfield"

682 SOMER: (read SOBER) John, Plainfield, yeoman 1/8/
    SOBER: 1780-2/8/1790 Barbara w. ch George, Jacob, Elizabeth, Susanna, Barbara
    (w of Peter Micheell) Catharina. Jacob Hubler Sr X. George Clewell, George
    Golkowsky, Joseph Clewell W
    Sober 172
    Sobert 377
    Soder 293
    Soller 64 774

683 SOLY: Daniel, Towamensing twp 6/8/1791-12/8/1791 w X. ch Daniel X, Peter, Con-
    rath X, Jacob, Paul, mens Margareth dau (w of Jost Dreisbach): and Mr Colver.
    Paul Grer, John Edmunds, Nathaniel Edmunds W. Codicil
    Solt 354
    Sommony 20

684 SOMMER: Michael, Easton 27/3/1759-27/4/1759 Elizabeth w. E. Roster, Lodowick
    Saumer W

685 SORBER: Jacob, Plainfield 6/5/1773-7/11/1774 Mary Engel W ch minors, Adam,
    Sarah, Jacob, Abraham, Christian, George, Elizabeth. Adam Sewer X, Casper
    Doll X.
    Sorber 168
    Sorbrich 697

686 SORVER: Adam, Chestnuthill twp 25/11/1790-12/2/1791 Nicholas Mittenberger, W.
    Kromer W

Sorver 109 549 624 635
Soull 760
Spangenberg 381 460 492 495 550 554 556 788
Spengler 481 773
Spingler 200
Spinner 670

687 SPONHEIMER: Henry, Plainfield, yeoman 23/1/1790-15/8/1797 Anna *Margaretha w X
ch Appolenia (w of Henry Stofflet), Ludwig; Peter Obershimer coX Francis J.
Smith, Valentine Boyer, Philip Achenbach W. (letters of admsn granted)
Spoonheimer 609
Springer 753
Stacher 143 202

688 STACKHOUSE: *Benjamin, Mt Bethel, yeoman 21/4/74-1/2/1776 Eleanor w X. ch
Rebecca, James, Sarah, Susanna. Sanders Miller co-X. Charles Scott and Joseph
Stackhouse W (junior)

689 STAHLNECKER: *George Up Milford, yeoman 21/4/86-7/4/1787 Mary Elizabet x. ch
Jacob X, John Adam X, Elizabeth (w of Peter Tice), Catherina, Barbara, Andrew,
Eve (w of John Rieser). Joseph Bishop, s of his dau Catharine. Jacob Smith,
Frederick Limbach Sr. Anthony Staehler W

690 STAHL: Jacob, Up Milford, yeoman 1/9/1786-30/9/86 ch Jacob X, Philip X, Abraham
et al Michael *Diehl, Henry *Diehl W

691 STAHL: George, Up Milford wheelright 30/4/1777-10/5/1777 Barbara w. ch John,
John-George. bros John, Jacob and Philip Stahl X. George Shautzenbuch, Jacob
Delb, Henry Weiss W
Stahl 120 169 283 300 558 778

692 STAHLER: Anthony. (?)-22/1/1798 Susanna and Nicholas Stahler X Philip Walter,
Nich Stahler W

693 STAHLER: Nicholas (?)-24/8/1795 David Strauss, Simon Schneyder W
Staehler 84 189 565 689
Stahly 83
Staler 18
Stalnecker 792

694 STAMBACH: Philip, Lynn twp 8/11/1776-(?) Christina w X. ch Daniel X, Jacob,
Philip, Anna-Elizabeth, Catharina (w of George Probst iss), Ann-Mary, Chris-
tina, Susanna. s sil John Probst, Philip Kuntz. Abraham beeli. George
Fausele W
Stauber 701 704

695 STAUFFER: *Daniel, Up Milford, yeoman 30/1/1790-1/5/1790 Catharine w. 2 s Abraham, Jacob. bil Abraham Stoutfer X & bil Jacob Gehman X. Jacob Probst,
George Kreibel W

696 STECHER: Melchoir, Forks, yeoman 13/9/1785-18/4/1786 ch Adam X, Lewis X, Matthew,
George, Henry, Christopher, Barbara (Wygant). lds in Mt Bethel. Joseph
Demuth, Wm Edmonds W. Codicil 28/4/1786 W by Rev Solomon Frederick
Stecher 457 520 611 619 639

697 STECKEL: Peter, Whitehall 30/6/1781-(?) Elizabeth w X. ch Henry and Jacob X,
John, Margaretta, Dorothea, Daniel. lds of Jacob Kohler, Peter Kohler,
Peter Burkhalter, Christian Seiger, Mardin Muckly, Joseph Balliet, John
Sorbrich, William Hoffman, Henry Yehl (in Heidelberg). Peter Kohler, George
Ramaly, Conrad Snyder W
Stedler 664
Steel 733
Steelsmith 230 275

Stefan 106
Stechler 447
698 STEHLY: *Christina, Bethlehem (?)-5/9/1795 ch Christian, Susanna, Frederick,
Johann, Christine, Catherine, Jacob. mens Maria and John Levering: Balbesa
Stehly: ld in Moore and Nazareth twps. Franz Thomas, Eve Lanius W Abraham
Levering X Anton Schmidt X
699 STEDDLY: Joseph, Lynn twp 24/4/1767-28/5/1767 ch Jacob, Elizabeth, Margaret
and younger s. mens Dewalt Kuntz trustee. Marri Wannemacher, Mathias Probst
and Joseph Steudel guar. Jacob Hoffman and Mathias Delong W
Stein 243
Steinberger 484
700 STEINER: Abraham, Shoeneck, Bethm twp Blacksmith 4/8/1781-10/9/1781 Salomey w
X. ch Abraham, Jacob, John, Elizabeth, Henry. bil August-Henrick Freeunke
coX. William Edmonds, Jacob Clewell W
701 STEINER: Peter, Bethlehem, wheelright 1/9/1795-9/6/1796 mens sis Magdalene (w of
Henry Frank of Shoeneck): Elizabeth Steiner dau of bro Henry: sis Elizabeth
bro Jacob Steiner: sis Barbara had dau (mar Johannes Heizof Salem N.C. bro
Henry Steiner had Peter: bro Abraham, decd had Abraham, John, Henry and
Elizabeth Hannah (w of Michael Knauss, had Abraham): John Heckenwelder of
Bethm (dad iss): Magdalene ("commonly called Magdalene Moor"). Golllieb
Stauber X, John Steiner of Plainfield X. Daniel Esterlein, Chr. Borhek,
John Hasse W
702 STEINER *Salome, Plainfield 7/11/1791-14/2/1793 ch John, Elizabeth, Henry,
Abraham. mens lds of August-Henry Frank, Abraham Steiner, late of Shoeneck
decd; John Dietrich. Jacob Eyerly jr X, Daniel Price X, John Hasse, George
Clewell W
703 STEIMER: *George, L Saucon, yeoman 27/8/1791-16/9/1791 Mary w X. ch Elizabeth,
Jacob, Christian, Margaut, Catharine, Magdalena. mens George Sterner "a ch
said to the charge of my s George decd" the ch of my dau Mary, decd Magdalena
and Elizabeth: lds of John Bruce, Daniel Geissinger, Valentine Opp. sil
Casmehr Hambt X. Jacob Koch, John Stout, George Butz W
704 STEINER: Elisabeth, Bethlehem, spinster 12/6/1800 "Gottlich Stauber, sil of my
bro Henry and Elizabeth his w dau of my said bro Henry" as X. bros Henry,
Jacob, Christian: Goddau Elizabeth dau of Abraham Levering: Elizabeth
Levering sis of Abraham Levering. Margaretha Metz, Abraham Levering W
Steiner 31 136 389 484 525 622
705 STEININGER: *George 27/2/1790-24/1/1791 Jacob Harman, George Guthsend (?) W
706 STEININGER: Leonard 1753-6/8/1753 Johannes Leichtenwalter. Andrew Heberly W
Steininger 18 603 641
Steinmann 254 598 764
Steinmetz 530
Steip 444 598
707 STEM: *Peter, Williams, yeoman 22/10/1795-14/12/1795 Anna Mary w X. and iss.
Isaac Shoemaker coX, John Koplin, Daniel Stem, Gottfried Raub W
708 STENSON: John, Mt Bethel 27/6/1770-4/8/1770 Mary w X. ch John, James, Robert,
Jennet, Sarah, Agness, Elizabeth, bro Archibald Gaston X. Samuel Betty, John
Moore, John Brown, William McFarren W
Stephen 371
Stepson 316
Stercher 155
Stern 361
Sterner 16 344 605 703 760

Stettin 195

709 STETTLER: Daniel 30/9/1788-8/11/1788 Philip Settler, Philip Petter X. Henry Geiger and Christian Schneider W

Stettler 270 366

710 STEUBEN: Conrad, Easton ?/1763-5/10/1765 Elizabeth Margaret w. sis Susanna-Catherine. J. Nich. Shnyder, John Dingler, D. Baehrringer W

Steuber 710

Steudel 699

711 STEVEN: Jacob 1/2/1760-15/3/1760 w. ch John-Adam, Catharina, John-Jacob, Elizabeth-Catharina, Susanna, Mary-Catharina. John Trexler, Christian Roth, William Bigel W

Steward 235 314

712 STIEFFER: Conrad (?)-23/6/1794 George Franz X John Serfass, Abraham Schupp W

713 STIEMER: Christian, Bethlehem 10/4/1787-30/4/87 Christn Ettwein, David Weinland, Carl Dreyspring

Stiner 700

714 STININGER: George, "the elder" Macungie 17/8/1761-20/1/1767 ch Christian X, George X, Mary, Margaret (Helbrich). gdch Henry and Christina ch of decd s Henry "and widow name Agat". gds George Berg s of dau Mary. John N. Moyer co-X. Michael Warmkeysel, Michael Klotz, Lewis Klotz W

Stitzelmeyer 597

715 STOCKER: Michael, Macungie 4/1/1771-24/1/1771 Margaret w X. ch Mary, Elizabeth, Catherine, Susanna, George et al. George Shitz co-X. Adam Gramus, Sebastian Truckenmiller W

** Stoeckel 256   Stofflet 687
** Stoehr 761   Stokesberry 311

716 STOLTZ: George, Plainfield 4/8/1764-19/8/1766 Elizabeth w ch Henry, Elizabeth, (w of Philip Shuck), Herman, Philip, Margaret (Dole), Catharina, George-Jacob. Philip Shuck and Philip Stoltz X. Jacob Sorber. Dil (Dielbauer)W

Stop 636

717 STORM: *Philip, Easton, labourer 14/7/1779-15/12/1779 Mary Elisabeth w X. John Bachman, Herman Shnyder, Michael Yohe W

Stotz 636

718 STOUT: *Peter, Plainfield, yeoman 27/7/1779-15/(read 27/10/1793-25/5/1795) Eve Elizabeth w. ch Christian, Joseph, (decd), Peter, Catherine (w of Nicholas Happel), Maria-Elizabeth (w of George Quier), Anna-Maria (w of Leonard Shertzer), Margaret (w of Jacob Raushenberger), Jannah (w of George Gerberich). William Henry Esq Nazareth X, Daniel Clewell, Nathaniel Clewell, Christopher Demuth W

Stout 24 81 103 144 338 407 438 528 703

Strachly 231

Straub 448

Straup 446

Strauss 125 267 387 659 693 80 719

Strein 124 125 273 351 563 571

Stroud 149 203 411 647 678 732

Stroup 144

Strouse 152

Stuber 331 371 448

Stumpff 17 612

Sutfin 98 122

Sutton 231

719 SWARTSWOOD: Minny, Delaware twp 16/7/1776-23/4/1777 moth Cornelia X. and
     Benjamin Shick brp. Abraham Curthright, Adam Shick, J. Chestnor W
720 SWARTSWORTH: Bernardus, Delaware twp 7/6/1773-24/3/1774 ch Margaret (Cole:
     dau Gennert), Jacob, Thomas, Elizabeth, Sarah (Custard: dau Margaret),
     Leah decd (had 5 ch, Anancy, Ostrone, Claudia Chambers, Famiky Cuthbright,
     Christopher Denmark), Anthony decd, Bernardus decd (had Samuel, Anthony,
     Benjamin, Moses, Gradus, all minors), Benjamin decd, Elizabeth, Mary (Mullen),
     mens gds Peter Swartsworth and his e Elizabeth: gddau Aunchy Mullen: gds
     Bernardus Denmark: gds Bernardus Swartsworth, eld s of Thomas: gdch Minny
     Swartsworth, minor: Hermonis Cole. Holm and Benjamin Depue X. Henry Cuth-
     right, William Ennes, John C. Symmes W. also mens friends John Brink and
     Manuel Gonsales
   ` Swartswood 117
     Swartz 152 466 500 591 788
721 SWEITZER: *John, Sr Bethlehem twp 31/7/1800-24/2/01 ch Andrew, Rudolph, John X,
     Leonard X, Elizabeth. mens ld of Anthony Dutler. Mathias Cress and Frederick
     Reichard W
     Swink 372
722 SYDER: Christian, "Machgunshie" 7/1/1769-5/6/1769 Cathrine w. ch Jacob, George,
     Catherine-Elizabeth X. mens "gds Christian Classy s of my eldest dau" Jacob
     Slough co-X. John Weaver, Michael Warmkessel W
**   Syder 47   Syderick 470
**   Sylface 39   Symmes 720
     Tapper 779
723 TAYLOR: Nathaniel, Allen 27/9/1764-4/3/1768 Jane(1) w X. ch John X, Sarah, Eliz-
     abeth, Mary m ld adj Archibald Laird. James Gray, Thos Boyd W
     Taylor 46 139
     Teel 471
     Teirich 195
     Teiss 193
     Tellefessen 32
     Templar 668
     Thomas 29 52 78 156 167 204 222 231 302 322 386 426 486 524 527 4 593 604 688
            744 759
     Thomason 59
     Thompson 471 479
     Thrane 8 630 631
     Tice 689
     Tillotson 539
     Tipfer 681
     Todd 223
     Toegli 105
     Tool 47 521
     Torney 187
     Toselman 288
     Townes 411
     Townsend 223
     Traill 6 11 80 277 326 343 385 391 402 411 412 416 475 534 569 587 593 655 781 793
     Transue 465 459 554 640
724 TRAXELL: *Nicholas, Whitehall, yeoman 2/7/1792-17/5/1797 Catherine w. ch Adam,
     Peter X, and 7 others. Peter (Sr and Jr) Rhoads, John Horn W
     Traxell 655

Treble 4

725 TREXLER: Peter Sr Macungie, husbandman 5/7/1787-10/4/1799 Catherine w. ch
Peter X, John X, Jonathan and 4 others. H. Brobst, John Romig W

726 TREXLER: John, Macungie, husbandman 26/1/1795-10/3/1795 Susanna w X. "stepch
to my youngest s to Jacob Hesler, Elizabeth Hesler which are prisoners by the
Indians, John Hesler, William Hesler, Anna Maria Hesler and my youngest s
Israel". ch Peter, Jeremiah, Emanuel, Ferdinand, Philipina (Albrecht),
Margaret (Kromer). John Jarret s of my dau Maria-Elizabeth decd. Jeremiah
Trexler (bro?). lds of Henry Haas, Jacob Heilman, Peter Sell, Peter Haff,
John Mohr: lds in Lowhill twp. John Kromer X. William Kromer jr, Jacob
Horner, Henry Haas W

Trexler 164 196 346 629 648 677 711 776

727 TRIBLE: George, L Saucon, farmer 6/8/1797-4/10/1797 Anna Elizabeth w X. ch
Peter et al. ld of Henry Allman decd. Isaac Shimer of Williams and Henry
Ohl of L Saucon X. Thomas McMullen, Michael Ernst W

Trollinger 648

Troxell 30 391 563 724

Trump 776

Tucker 22

Turner 227

Turny 317

Ueberroth 331

728 UHLER: *Henry, Forks, singleman 1/8/1793-2/8/94 moth Mary Magdalena. bros
Jacob, Valentine, Andrew X. sis Margaret (w of Charles Reymer), Elizabeth
(w of John Oberly) Anthony Oberly and Michael Smith W

Uhler 37

729 UNANGST: *Bastian, Bethlehem twp yeoman 16/3/93-11/11/1793 Elizabeth w X. ch
Henry, Casper X, Catharina. lds of Nicholas Kramer, Jacob Shleppy. Johannes
Deobald, Christian Debald and Joseph Sheber W

Unangst 304 315 492 554

730 UTTLY: Elizabeth (?)-20/1/1789 Andreas Borhek X Christ. Herning X. Christ
Ettwein, Danl Kleist W

Vanables 424

Vanaken 464

Vanbuskirk 316

731 VAN CAMPEN: Benjamin, L Smithfield 7/3/1789-27/10/1789 Rachael w X. mens bro
John had s Abraham: "9 slaves to be freed at age of 28". lds in Valpack
twp Sussex. Nicholas Depue Esq X. John Lanterman (Sr Jr), Philip Shrawder W

Van Campen 432 652 733

732 VAN DER MARK: John, L Smithfield 13/9/1788-28/10/1788 Janney w X. ch Abraham,
Jeremiah X, John, Moses, Daniel, Janney (w of Abraham Cosan), lds of James
Schoenover, Jacobus Vangarten Co-X, Jacob Stroud, Joseph Mantango, Francis
Smith and Benjamin Schoenover W

Van der Mark 96 97 98 735

** Van Dike 112   Van Erd 51 171 585
** Van Etten 112   Van Etter 431
** Van flerd 678   Van Garten 732

733 VAN GORDON: Jacobus, Delaware, farmer 13/2/1796-25/2/1796 Catherine w. ch
Moses X, Isaac, Abraham, David, Susanna (w of John van Campen), Mary (w of
Parafine Jones), Elizabeth (w of John Henry), Catherine (w of Solomon
Rosekrantz). Henry Steel, Alexander van Gordon jr Joseph Chestnor W

Van Gordon 111

Van Keiren 735

734 VAN VLECK: Henry, late of New York, now of Bethlehem, merchant. 3/12/1784-
5/2/1785 ch Isaac of Phila, merchant, Jacob of Bethm clerk, Henry of Litiz,
hatter, Abraham (had Laurence, Henry, Judith, Maria-Elizabeth), Mary (w of
Emanuel Mitschman), Elizabeth dil widow of Abraham. Abraham Andreas, silver-
smith, Christian R. Heckenwelder, John Okely, Wilhelm Boehler W, Thomas
Bartow of Phila merchant, James H. Kip of New York, and 3 s Isaac, Jacob and
Henry Van V. and sil Emanuel Nitschman X
Van Vleck 22 55 359 439 512 738

735 VAN VLEET: Dirck, L Smithfield, farmer 25/5/1774-16/11/1774 Rachael w. ch Dirck
X, Goertz, Marztye-Judith, Anna-Cathatina, Dirk van Keuren Jenneke, Elizabeth,
Rachael, Lidia, Joseph, Cornelia. Daniel Depue of Walpeck X. Garret Brod-
head, John Van der Mark, Daniel Depue W
Van Vleet 149
Van Vliet 117 463
Verbis 358

736 VERDRIESS: *Anna Catharina, Bethlehem (?)-10/8/1801 Peter Youngman. Geotge
Huber, David Wineland W Daniel Kleist X
Versislow 495
Vetter 302
Vettertive 524

737 VOLLMAN: Melchoir, Macungie, yeoman 3/12/1785-22/9/1789 Maria Barbara w. "2 yet
living ch Melchior and Mary Barbara (w of John Wurtz)" Michael Shaffer of
Macungie X. Frederick Limbach, George Reiss, Christian Fisher W
Vogt 50 522 640
Volck 514
Vollert 75 375 755
Von Erd 297

738 VON MARSCHALL: *Anne, Bethlehem (sig Anna Dorothea) ?/8/1795-23/2/1796 mens
neph and niece Fredk-Christian X and Johanna-Elizabeth von Schweinitz: Rosina
Schultze: Wilhelm-Heinrich van Vleck: Jacob van Vleck: Elizabeth Lewis:
Hans-Christian von Schweinitz X Jacob v. Vleck, Elizabeth Lewis W

739 WAGENER: David, Easton, Esquire 18/2/1796-7/6/1796 Susanna w. ch David, Abraham,
Daniel X, John X, Elizabeth, Deborah, Mary: daus Elizabeth (w of Jacob
Meixsell), Mary (w of Christian Butz), Deborah (w of Adam Deshler). held ld
in partnership. with Jacob Weiss. John Arndt guar of Abraham. John Mulhollen,
John Herster, Jacob Opp W. (see Eyerman's Genealogical Studies)
Wagener 554 647
Waggoner 7 186

740 WAGNER: Anthon, Macungie (?)-12/1/1787 John Ettwein X. Peter Butz, Henry Romig
W
Wagner 5 123 240 337 385 421 448

741 WAHL: John Michael (?)-10/11/1801 Christopher Hartung X W. Lewis Encke W
Waldman 700 (perhaps Waidman)

742 WALBERT: George, Macungie (?)-13/12/1799 Peter and George Walbert X. Henry
Romich, Jacob Romich W

743 WALKER: John, Allen twp 4/6/1777-17/6/1777 ch William X, John X, Jane (w of
John Hays), Ann, Mary-Ann. Mary King, William McNair, William Carruthers W
Walker 102 347 433 440 567
Wallace 758

744 WALTER: *Bernat, Forks, farmer 2/6/1780-2/6/80 Eve w. ch Conrad, John, Barnet,
Catherine, Michael, George, Hannah (w of Jeremiah Kock), Mary (w of Jacob
Bress), Elizabeth (w of William Thomas), Christina (wid of Fredk Peyser).
Jacob Shoemaker X, John and Abraham Arndt W

745 WALTER: Philip, Macungie 6/9/1765-4/7/1766 Mary-Dorothea w. ch Philip, Christiana
    Belena-Elizabeth. Jacob Herman X, Mary-Dorothea w X. Johannes Baere,
    Johannes Diependerfer, Sebastian Truckenmiller W
    Walter 50 646 692
    Waltman 172
    Walton 557 749
746 WANDEL: Tobias, Up Milford, sievenaker 10/9/88-26/10/1791 Agnes-Catharina w.
    ch Agnes-Maria, Elizabeth (w of Leonhart Lautenshlaeger). Andreas Giering
    and James Gill both of Emaus X. Martin Leibert, Ludwig *Andreas Henry Bauer W
747 WANNEMACHER: *George (?)-6/1/1795 Lewis Encke, Johannes Heneke, Frederick
    Peiffer W
    Wannemacher 253 543 637 699 772
    Ward 656 675
    Warman 123
748 WARMKESSEL: Frederick, Allen, yeoman 3/10/1792-16/1/1793 Susanna w and ch.
    Theobald Albrecht, Nicholas Krammer, Peter Rhoads, Cond Haein W
    Warmkessel 714 722
749 WARNER: Daniel, Gnadenhuetten on Manony Creek. Bethia w decd. ch Samuel, Esra,
    Massa X, Hannah, Daniel, John, Mary (w of Elisha Smith). Boaz Walton and
    Peter Edmunds W
    Warner 148
750 WARRIG: *Valentine, L Saucon, farmer 20/7/1780-25/10/1783 Mary w X. ch all
    minors, Simon, Ludwig et al. Ludwig and Christopher Heller W
    Wasser 510
    Wassum 208
751 WASSUM: Conrad, Heidelberg, yeoman and sergeant in Co. under command of Nicholas
    Wetterholt of 1st bat. Penn Reg 22/1/1757-28/5/1759 Anna-Margaretha w X.
    mens bros John, Leonard, George, lds of John Rhoads, John Geiger, George and
    Jacob Rex W
    Wayall 615
752 WEAVER: Henry, Up Saucon, yeoman 29/3/1796-6/4/1796 Margareth w. ch John,
    Michael, Jacob, Ann-Catherine, Henry, Peter, Joseph, David, Margareth. Philip
    Paul of L Saucon and Abraham Seyder of Up Saucon X. John Hasse, Jno-Frederick
    Rudolph, Mathias Zeisloff W
753 WEAVER: Erhart, Up Saucon, weaver 18/11/1789-14/4/1795 Magdalena w. ch George-
    Adam X, Jonas X, Michael, Margaret (w of Conrad Rone), Elias, Christina (w of
    Martin Rishel), Magdalene (w of "one"Donner), Henry, Sophia, Catherine (late
    w of Daniel Springer) ch Jonathan and Isaac Springer: Abraham Seyder, Ph.
    Scherre W
754 WEAVER: *Magdalna, wid of Jacob of Bucks 1/7/86-22/6/1790 Jonas Hertzel X. mens
    sil William Yonson. Jacob Ertman, George Krieber W
755 WEAVER: George L Saucon 28/7/1770-3/9/1770 Anna Barbara w ch Valentine, Cath-
    erine, Ann-Mary. Valentine Opp X. Math. Der, Jost Vollert W
756 WEAVER: Jacob, 30/1/1761-11/8/1761 Anna Catherine w. ch Jacob et al Christian
    Smith, Michael Ohl, Henry Geiger W
757 WEAVER: *Jacob (?)-11/8/1761. John Dietrich, Bald. Dauff, Michael Ohl, Christi
    Smith W
758 WEAVER: *Christian Mt Bethl 29/3/1783-27/3/83? Barbara w ch Jacob X, Moses,
    Rosinna, (w of Sam Noy), Elizabeth (w of Joseph Wallace), Mary (w of Daniel
    Lewis), Charity (w of Robt Campbell), Eve Jane (w of John Miller). William
    McFarren co-X. Nathaniel Brittain, William Rea. Adriejean Aten
    Weaver 106 193 233 245 292 297 344 444 529 568 593 630 631 722 (see Weber)

759 WEBER:＊ Andrew, Bethlehem: "house-father of Children's Oeconomies" (prob 1784)
      w. X. mens Thos. Bartow: cous Christian Eggert X and Thomas Bartow guar of
      Ch;oec; latter rem. to Phila and Francis Thomas loc. ten. X mens 3 ch. John
      Jungmann, John Wygand W.
760 WEBER: *Jacob, Allen farmer Margareth w. mens dau Catherine (w of Henry Fet-
      zinger of Allen and had Margaret, George, Jacob, John, Catherine) Nicholas
      Scull, decd surveyor: lds of Valentine Waldmna, Nicholas Rummel, Hannis
      Sterner, James Young, George Beck, Robert Young, Nicholas Sterner: William
      Asterlee gave decd (12/2/1765). Jacob Geissinger, blacksmith, and his s
      George X. John Hasse, Nicholas Rumel W (17/6/1790-12/7/1790)
761 WEBER (von): Henry, Sr Up Saucon, yeoman 6/1/83-31/3/1783 ch Henry X, Hannes of
      Allen, Michael of Maxetawny, Elizabeth (w of Henry Reitz), Sarah (w of Leonard
      Reichert), Casper of Allentown. mens 3 ch of dau Susanna by lst hus Jacob
      Beyer and 2 ch by 2d hus Hannes Groten: mens dau Hannah (w of Joseph
      Hornecker). Adam Romig co-X. John Hasse, Peter Stochr. W
      Weber 174 199 211 752 (see Weaver)
762 WEHR: Simon 1787-10/4/1799 Christian Schneider, John Henry Helfuch. Philip
      Pretz W
      Wehr 78 207 538 790
      Weidknecht 371
      Weidler 358
763 WEIDMAN: Henry, Up Mt Bethel, yeoman 10/5/1792-29/4/1793 Anna Mary w. ch Jacob,
      Philip, Daniel, Catherine, Mary. mens sil Jacob and Daniel X. Jno Faunce,
      Jacob Dietterich, James *Green W
      Weidman 553
764 WEIGANDT: Cornelius, Easton, yeoman 26/7/1796-14/1/1800 ch John X, Jacob X,
      Peter, Cornelius, Hannah (w of Conrad Best), Maria-Agnetta decd (w of Henry
      Fraess iss), Susanna (w of Peter Ihrick.) William Henry, Joachim Wigman W
      Weigand 142 457 513 759
      Weigman 539
765 WEINLAND: Philipina, wid of Nicholas, Bethlehem 31/1/1785-8/12/1790 ch David X,
      Johannes, Elizabeth. mens George Loesch. John Elewell co-X Joseph Otto, William
      Henry W
      Weinland 51 127 713 768
766 WEIS: Jacob, L Saucon 23/2/1770-(?) Anna Margaret w X. and ch. Adam Luckenbach,
      Matthew Riegel and Jacob Giesie W
      Weisel 332
767 WEISER: Christopher, Salisbury, yeoman 27/4/68-6/7/1768 Maria Catharina w. ch
      John X, Jacob X, Benjamin, Frederick, Margareth (w of Robar Cane), Elizabeth
      (w of Philip Broudanbock), Anne (w of Adam Lash) "ch only by my first w". ld
      bt of Sebastian Knous and George Klein. S. Knauss, Andrew Giering, George A.
      Hahn W
768 WEISS: Matthias, Bethlehem 2/10/1795-5/11/1795 ch John X, Catharine(w of Fredk
      Blum of Hope, Sussex Co N.J.), John-George X, Pauluas, Mathias. mens dil Anna
      Maria w of s John: gdch Mathias-Frederick and Mary Blum: gds David Weiss s of
      John-George. Daniel Kleist, David Weinland, Christian Eggert W
769 WEISS: *Benedict 28/3/1757-14/6/1757 Silvester Holbe et al W
770 WEISS: *Benedict, Weisenberg 28/3/1757-(?) ch Peter and 3 dau. Andreas Reiss,
      Christian Miller, Silvester Holbe, Nicholas Kempp W
      Weiss 56 313 217 299 426 439 598 634 649 691 739
      Weissinger 328
      Weitner 342

771 WEITZEL: *Jacob, Lynn 27/8/1780-(?) Susanna w X ch John-Martin, Jacob et al.
   Martin Wertman co X George Breisch, Mathias Probst W mens lds of Geo Breisch,
   Henry Rubrecht, Leonard Billman
772 WEITZEL: *Martin ?/11/1762-20/4/1764 Mark Vanamaker jr. and George Hermany W
   Weitzel 635
773 WELDN: Philip, Moore twp 16/1/1796-15/2/1796 Joseph Larosh, Christian Spengler W
   Welter 193
   Weller 751
774 WELTZ: Andreas, Up Saucon, yeoman 15/8/1765-24/10/1765 bros John-George, George.
   sis Appolonia (w of Casper Brener decd). Henry Rumfelt X. Philip Soller,
   Conrad Reigle W
   Wench 364 649
   Wentz 597
775 WENTZEL (?)
   Werks 18
   Werner 173 214 798
   Werst 578
   Wertman 191 771
   Wertz 316 792
   Wesgo 565
   Weshgo 316
   Westfall 111
   Westgo 396
   Wetterholt 191
776 WETZEL: Jacob, Up Milford 27/1/1773-30/5/1774 ch Peter, Jacob, John, Ann-Mary
   (w of Adam Trump) Barbara (w of Christian Miller). gddau Margaret Hawk, Henry
   Kocker, Jacob Stahl, Leonard Gephart W
777 WETZELL: Catharina, Macungie 8/12/1767-4/2/1768 ch John X, Henry, Jacob, Cath-
   arina (w of Isaac Jarreth), Magdalena, Maria. gds John Adam Romich s of decd
   dau Bennigal w of John Romick, Michael Schmayer, Lewis Klotz W
778 WETZELL: Conrad, Macungie, husbandman 5/3/1753-17/5/1753 Anna Catherine w X. ch
   Johannes, Catherine, Henry, Magdalena, Bernhard (f), Anna-Maria Ludwig Klotz,
   Jacob Ernhardt, Sebastian H Knous W
   Wetzel 55 193 332 337 387 659
   Weygandt 136
   White 443 545 678
   Whiteman 656
   Whits 22
   Wicant 129
779 WIEDER: Adam, Salisbury: "old and weak" 16/1/98-23/1/1798 Hans-Adam X, John,
   Michael, Valentine X, Casper, Lodwig, Margaret(w of Henry Koon), Elizabeth (w
   of John Tapper), Mary-Elizabeth (w of Doria Dorias Asch), Eve (w of Christian
   Heyberger). Henry Kooken, Martin Ritter, Ludwig Klotz W
   Wieder 187
780 WIEDERSTEIN: Henry, Lynn twp (?)-25/8/1800 Adam Kuntz X. George Creutz, Jacob
   Oswald W
   Wiegman 764
   Wiesman 656
   Wiessinger 190
   Wiester 450
   Wigman 91 226 601
   Wild 13

781 WILHELM: Michael, Forks 24/9/1776-13/8/1777 mens eld bro Jacob; Mary dau of
    Elizabeth Nicholson: bro Frederick; ld of Jacob Wilhelm. Uncle Fredk.
    Kuhn X. Henry Fullert, Hy Barnet, Robert Traill W
    Wilhelm 11 385 457
    Willauer 275
    Williams 99 133 387 678
782 WILSON: Samuel, Allen, yeoman 4/12/1796-6/3/1797 Sarah w. ch Sarah (w of Wm
    Mulhollen), Abigail Mary, Elizabeth, Abraham, Hugh. Elizabeth Buckman,
    servant. lds of Hugh Horner, George Wolf, John Brown, John Wilson. s Abra-
    ham, s Hugh and George Palmer X. John Wilson, James Horner W
    Wilson 59 269 301 401 403 433 479
    Winchester 229
    Wind 493 559
783 WINELAND: John Nicholas, Gnadenthall, Bethlehem twp yeoman 11/12/1776-19/8/1783
    Philippina w X ch John, Mary, Christina, Elizabeth, David, bil Jacob Loesch
    and Hermanus Loesch co-X George Hartman, J. Michael Zalm, Peter Mohrdick W
    Winland 423
    Winsch 377 279
784 WINTER: Jacob, Weisenberg 28/12/1770-14/5/1773 Anna Mary w X. mens Anna-Mary
    (dau ?) w of Jost Meyer of Whitehall: the ch of George Winter, late of York
    Co. George Sassamanhausen of Maxatawny, Berks X. Melchr Seib, Geo. Gutekunst W
    Wireland 736
785 WISSINGER: Jacob 20/7/1790-2/9/1790 Andreas Borhek, John Hasse, Henry Lindenmeyer
    W
    Witman 54 177
    Witner 478
786 WOLF: George, Bethlehem twp 20/7/1790-2/9/1790 George Beck, Mathias Koenig W
787 WOLF: Henry, 1766-27/12/1766 w and 5 ch incl Philip, John Berger and Christian
    Fuchs Easton W
** Wolf 369   Woolf 73 227
** Wolfgang 753   Woolley 615
** Wolfgouch 375   Wortman 349
** Wood 229 650   Wurtz 737
** Woodring 297 650   Wyant 557
** Wooleving 297   Wygant 345 696
788 YEAGER: John, Forks, yeoman 2/4/1796-23/5/1796 Elizabeth w. ch John, Henry X,
    Philip X, Christian, Mary, Catherine, Eve, Elizabeth, Margareth. mens lds of
    Geo-William Roup, Widow Moser, Lawrence Swarts et al. Isaac *Koon, John
    Spangenberger, John Odenwelder W
    Yeager 495
789 YEAKEL: *Baltzer, Up Milford, yeoman 2/10/1797-27/12/1797 Susanna w. ch David X,
    Andrew, Rosina, Sarah, Barbara; bro Melchoir Yeakel co-X Battzer Krauss, George
    Kriebel W
790 YEGAR: John, Heidelberg 7/8/1766-28/8/1766 Julianna w. ch John, Adam. mens
    Michael Ohl. Ph. Ebert, Jacob Arndt, Heidelberg. Simon Wehr W
    Yeht 697
791 YODER: Casper, Up Saucon, yeoman 17/4/1798-5/10/1798 Fronia w. ch John X, Jacob,
    Anna (w of Jacob Moyer), Molly (w of Christian Shimel), Susanna, Fromid,
    Barbara ld in Springfield twp. bro Abraham Yoder co X Peter Meyer, Samuel
    Meyer W
    Yoder 502 674
    Yohe 30 80 391 409 655 717 793

Yonson 754
Yooran 115
792 (see Addenda No 803)
793 YOUNG: *Henry, Easton, locksmith 20/7/1785-22/9/1785 Anna Elizabeth w. ch
John, Sophia (w of George Dreisbach), Catherine (decd had iss); Abraham Labar
of Easton, tailor X, Robert Traill, Michael Yohe, Christian Holland W
794 YOUNG: James, Allen, yeoman 9/1/1765-1/3/1765 Ester w. ch William. mens sis
Elizabeth Boyd (and iss): sis Mary Young: cous James Orr: Rev Mershel
trustee: bro Robt. Young and Thomas Boyd X. Thomas and Daniel Runsicker W
795 YOUNG: William, yeoman 3/11/1753-20/3/1754 Elizabeth w. ch Robert, William,
Alexander, Mary, James X, Elizabeth (had 2 ch William and Elizabeth).
Thomas Armstrong co-X, Robert Gregg, overseer: George Gibson, James Calwell W
Young 10 60 143 266 276 325 405 445 470 568 587 760
Youngsberg 104 185 254 413 457 503
Youngman 156 378 422 736 759
Yumig 402
796 YUND: *Dorothea, wid of Jacob, Whitehall 16/3/1780-(?) George, Daniel X, Abra-
ham, Mary, Peter (eldest), Jacob (?). mens son's w Eve-Catherine, Philip-
Jacob Schriber co-X. Michael Kolb, Stephen Schnyder W
Zahn 783
797 ZIEGLER: John Frederick, Nazareth, husbandman. 19/3/1785-4/8/1786 Catherine
w X. ch John-Fredk, Mary-Catherine (w of Andreas Birte) William Edmonds,
Martin Boehner W
Ziegler 529
798 ZEINER: *George, L Saucon, yeoman 12/11/1787-7/4/1788 Anna w X. ch George,
Barbara. stepch Jacob and Margaret Kuntzman. Frederick Werner, Peter Lean W

Ziegler 248 377 676	Zeisberger 8
Ziegenfuse 552	Zeisloff 752
Zieglerfuss 529	Zeller 312 640
Zimmerman 662	Zerfass 341
Zug 587	Zerfink 523

ADDENDA:

799 BEYER: William, Plainfield 17/8/1766-1/10/1767 Margaret w. ch Margareth, Catherine, Christina, Barbara, Lennert Beyer, John-Geo Bernhard W
800 HOEFFELFINDER (see No 294)
801 SHAFER: John, Hamilton sts (?)-25/4/1801 George Shaffer and Henry Hauser X
mens Leonard Diehl. John Strauss and David Strauss W
802 LANIUSS: Eve, Bethlehem (?)-23/10/1801 John Schropp and Abraham Smith X
Abraham Huebner and Joseph Oerter W
803 OLLENWEIN: Yost, Up Milford twp 15/8/1763-17/10/1763 Eve w. ch Andrew X, John,
Mary-Elizabeth (w of George Stalnecker), Eve (w of Felix Hoover), Anna-
Elizabeth (w of Jacob Kaylor), Anna-Barbara. Andrew Engelman, Adam Kortz and
Peter Wertz W

PAGE	WILL NUMBER	
1	7	Omit 12/3/1764
2	21	Omit Philip WALTER
7	64	read to Henry
7	68	read 30/6/1792
7	69	omit Chris-
9	81	read 3/9/1793-16/9/1794
10	94	for ld of Jacob Juncker read Martin Conrad
30	294	for Christian Bestch read Bertsch
45	445	for Gottlief read Gottlob
45	448	for *George read John
47	470	last name on will should be George Clauss W
60	601	read 11/8/1790 - 13/7/1792
62	635	read Shallenberger
64	648	read 648 instead of YRI
68	687	read Peter Obershimer
69	699	read Steidly
69	701	read Johannes Reiz of
69	702	read 7/11/1791 - 14/2/1795
75	764	read Joachim Wiegman
77	782	read Elizabeth Ruckman

www.ingramcontent.com/pod-product-compliance
Lightning Source LLC
Chambersburg PA
CBHW020558030426
42337CB00013B/1137